W9-BKU-255

A Hop, Skip, and a Jump
Through the Bible

J. Ellsworth Kalas

A *Hop,* *Skip,* and a *Jump* Through the Bible

Abingdon Press
Nashville

A HOP, SKIP, AND A JUMP THROUGH THE BIBLE

Library of Congress Cataloging-in-Publication Data

Kalas, J. Ellsworth, 1923-
A hop, skip, and a jump through the Bible / J. Ellsworth Kalas.
    p. cm.
ISBN 978-0-687-64446-9 (binding: pbk. : alk. paper)
1. Bible—Introductions.   I. Title.

BS475.3.K35 2007
220.6′1—dc22

2007021970

07 08 09 10 11 12 13 14 15 16—10 9 8 7 6 5 4 3 2 1

MANUFACTURED IN THE UNITED STATES OF AMERICA

To all those people who love the Bible,
but love too little of it,
in the hope that they will come to love
their favorite portions still better
when they see how the whole grand Book comes together.

Contents

Foreword

A GREAT MANY YEARS AGO, DURING MY FIRST YEAR AS SENIOR PASTOR AT the Church of the Savior in Cleveland, Ohio, I celebrated the Lenten season by leading a special Sunday evening Bible study. I had come to realize that in all the churches I had known there were many people, women and men, younger and older, who participated in Bible studies, but that most of those Bible studies were concentrated on a particular book or section of the Bible, or on some biblical topic. As a result, most of these people had a very disjointed knowledge of the Bible—a little of Genesis, something of the Psalms, the Gospel of John and the Epistle to the Romans—but with no sense of the relationship of these bits and pieces, and surely no sense of what I like to call "the Grand Plot" of the Bible.

So I set out on those Sunday evenings of Lent to take my voluntary study group from Genesis to Revelation. I called it "A Walk Through the Bible."

But Sally Baldwin, who had chaired the Lenten planning, saw it another way. When the administrative body of the church met not long after Lent, to discuss the life of the church and its activities, Sally reported on the Lenten programming. She said, "Dr. Kalas called this Lenten study 'A Walk Through the Bible.' I found it to be more of a hop, skip, and jump."

I liked what Sally said. She was reporting that the study had been lively and enjoyable, with opportunities to smile and even to laugh. That's as it ought to be, because the Bible is a lively book, lively twice over, in fact: lively in its stories and insights, and lively in the life it brings to those who take it seriously.

Since then I have done this "Hop, Skip, and a Jump" scores and scores of times, sometimes in half-a-dozen lectures over several days, and sometimes in a whirlwind forty-five minutes. Now I have finally tried to put it into a book. I hope you will enjoy the trip, whether you find it a walk or a hop-skip-jump. Especially, I hope you will see the Bible as a grand, eternal plot, and that you will find your place under God in this plot.

— J. Ellsworth Kalas

1

In the Beginning, God

Genesis

ONCE UPON A TIME, THERE WAS GOD. AND THAT'S ALL THERE WAS. That's the way the book of Genesis leads us into the Grand Eternal Plot. Since perhaps you are a postmodern reader, you may want to remind me that my opening statement isn't scientific. You're quite right. The book of Genesis isn't meant to be scientific or anti-scientific, because ultimately God isn't an issue of science. For those who believe, God is an issue of faith and experience, so also God is the issue of life, of purpose and meaning, and of everything else that is strategic to life at its best. That's why the story begins as it does, with God, because there's no other place to begin. As the biblical story unfolds, we soon realize that not only does it begin with God; in its entirety, it is God's story. Even when God isn't mentioned, God is still the brooding presence, wonderfully and sometimes fearfully inescapable.

Perhaps another question has occurred to you. You are wondering who made God. I don't want to be difficult, but you've missed the point. Nobody made God; if someone or something had made God, then that one or that thing would be God.

So when the story begins, God is there and that's it. That's where the book of Genesis starts, and in truth it's hard to improve on such a beginning. The ancient writer saw God as the root and base of everything, and announced this conviction with disarming directness and simplicity. "In the beginning when God created the heavens and the earth, the earth was a formless void and darkness covered the face of the deep, while a wind from God swept over the face of the waters" (Genesis 1:1-2). The writer is so comfortable with what he is reporting that he finds no need for explanation on the one hand or for "isn't it wonderful!" on the other. This is the way it happened, so the writer is satisfied simply to report the facts.

The next detail in the story is very special; so special because of the beautiful thing it tells us about God. As God begins bringing order to the "formless void and darkness," the order comes by way of conversation. Not a bombast of activity or a marshaling of divine troops, but a conversation: "Then God said, 'Let there be light'; and there was light" (Genesis 1:3). The rest of the Creation story unfolds in the same fashion: God speaks, and it happens. I like that. It means that by nature God is a communicator, so in love with what is being made as to talk with it. I know, from this moment in the opening verses of Genesis, that prayer makes sense, because God is a communicator and can be talked with. Perhaps Genesis is describing the big bang of science, or perhaps it is seeking only to introduce us to what Scriptures call the "still small voice" (1 Kings 19:12 RSV). Whatever, it reminds me that God is a communicator, and I like that.

And I'm glad that at each step in the Creation story, "God saw that it was good." As I look out of my window on trees that are just beginning to tingle with spring, I agree that it's good. I like this world God gave us, and I'm dreadfully sorry for the things we've done to mess it up.

When planet Earth and the expanding universe were ready, "God created humankind in his image, / in the image of God he created them; / male and female he created them" (Genesis 1:27). From our point of view, this is where the plot really begins, because the Bible is the story of God's relationship with our human race. Now, I confess that sometimes I don't feel too good about the human race in general and about myself in particular. At such times I remind myself that we are made in God's image. Whatever may have happened to us in the meanwhile, basically we're made of good stuff. In fact, very, very good stuff. With that in mind, I should never give up on the human race, or you, or myself.

A few verses into the story, the writer (or *writers,* if you prefer) adds a kind of commentary on our human creation. He tells of God making man "from the dust of the ground," and breathing into that dust "the breath of life" (Genesis 2:7). Then the writer tells us that in this world where everything was "good," God saw one thing that was not good: "It is not good that the man should be alone" (Genesis 2:18). You and I are social creatures. We like our times of solitude, and we need them—some more and some less—but we were meant for community. Specifically, it is at this point in the Genesis story that we are introduced to marriage and the family.

But as I said a moment ago, we humans have messed up our planet. It is just here that the plot thickens. A "crafty" stranger approaches Adam and Eve. His approach is clever; there is no confrontation, just a question: "Did God say, 'You shall not eat from any tree in the garden'?" (Genesis 3:1). You could read half-a-hundred poems, stories, and novels about sin and hear twice as many sermons, and you wouldn't find more about the nature of temptation and sin than in this story of the serpent's visit with Adam and Eve. Once the serpent has raised a question in the listener's mind about the character of God, the circuitous trip to trouble becomes a beeline. At the same time, however, it is in this questioning that we can come to know more of the wonder of God's character. The questioning itself is not so much the issue as the spirit in which we do it and the choices we then make.

Temptation reaches us through two key elements of our wonderful humanness: we are free moral agents, and we want to believe in something. Choice is our middle name. Making choices is as native to us as breathing; no wonder yes and no are such early words in our vocabulary, and the gestures for those two words are among the earliest we employ. You and I are choosers by nature, because we are—as I said a moment ago—free moral agents.

So, too, we want something to believe in. This is the fabric around which our personalities take shape. What we are as time goes by is not simply a matter of the people we meet and the things that happen to us, but what we believe. At the same time, of course, what we believe is in large part a product of the people and happenings of our lives. And this believing is not limited to the big questions about God and eternal destiny, but also includes the little questions that stem from and feed into the big ones—questions such as how we choose to treat people and to respond to circumstances, for instance—the smaller kinds of questions that are the stuff of our everyday lives.

Well, Adam and Eve made a choice, and they made it on the basis of a belief. They believed in the questions the serpent raised rather than what they had already experienced of the goodness of God, and on that basis they made a choice. It was a bad one, and Adam and Eve learned (as we do) that choices always have consequences. Further, they learned that these consequences are never limited to the persons who make them.

It seems to me that for Adam and Eve, the worst of the consequences was the alienation that came (and continues to come) with sin. By nature (that is, by creation) Adam and Eve, being made in God's image, were inclined toward God. But having sinned, they "hid themselves from the presence of the LORD God" (Genesis 3:8). By nature, Adam and Eve were indissolubly tied to one another; Adam had described Eve as "bone of my bones / and flesh of my flesh" (Genesis 2:23). Having sinned, however, Adam turned on the one closest to him: "The woman whom you gave to be with me, she gave me fruit from the tree, and I ate" (Genesis 3:12). Indeed, these humans became estranged from themselves. In their original state, they "were both naked, and were not ashamed" (Genesis 2:25). But afterwards, they were uncomfortable looking upon themselves, so they made fig leaves to hide themselves from themselves.

These results of sin are not described as judgments from God. They seem rather to be nothing other than the fruit of wrongful conduct: plant crabgrass seed and you will get crabgrass. We do well to keep this in mind when we evaluate the happenings in our lives. People sometimes say, when certain predictable misfortunes come upon them, "God must be punishing me," when in some such instances we are, in truth, punishing ourselves. That is, we're getting the crop we should expect from the seed we've sown.

So at this point the plot of our story gets painfully complicated. We never sin simply to ourselves, and we are never righteous simply to ourselves; whatever we are, for good or ill, we *share* it with others. Adam and Eve have a son. Eve has such high hopes for him that she names him Cain, meaning "gotten" or "produced," because she said, "I have produced a man with the help of the LORD" (Genesis 4:1). Adam and Eve have another son, named Abel. When the boys are grown, Cain becomes a farmer and Abel a herdsman. Jealousy grows between them—at least on Cain's part—so that when they make their offerings to God, Cain's resentment deepens and he murders his brother. If you have any instinct (of course you do) for the way we humans live and for what happens to us, you realize that this tragic family murder is as much the child of Adam and Eve's sin as the two boys are the children of their parents' union. The tragedy is terribly sad, but not terribly surprising.

The next several chapters of Genesis are heavily overcast, with only occasional bursts of sunlight. Having lost both their sons—Abel to death and Cain to the life of a fugitive—Adam and Eve must have felt that life outside Eden was nothing but disaster. But God extended grace: they were given another son, Seth, and with him the promise of a new line. But it is only a matter of time until this new line is as corrupt as the line coming from Cain. So corrupt, in fact, that God "saw that the wickedness of humankind was great in the earth, and that every inclination of the thoughts of their hearts was only evil continually." The situation was so grievous to God that "the LORD was sorry that he had made humankind on the earth" (Genesis 6:5-6).

And yet, the cause was not wholly lost. In the midst of such evil, like a violet pushing its way through a crack in an asphalt parking lot, there was Noah: "A righteous man, blameless in his generation; Noah walked with God" (Genesis 6:9). This sentence makes me rise up out of my chair, even as I write. I can understand sin and depravity, and how easily it passes from person to person and generation to generation; what I cannot understand—short of the grace and mercy of God—is the way purity, beauty, goodness, and godliness continue to appear, even under the most hopeless of circumstances.

As Genesis reports it, judgment comes upon the earth by way of a flood. Rain not only falls from the skies, but the springs of the earth erupt from below. All that is saved is Noah and his family, a company of eight, and a starter team for earth's animal kingdom. I need to mention that as Genesis tells the story, the animal kingdom suffers as a result of the sins of the human race. This seems quite unfair, but you'll notice that it's still going on. As we humans mistreat our planet, the rest of nature suffers for our sins—sometimes, in fact, to the extinction of particular elements of nature.

I wish I could tell you that everything was good after our human race got its new start with the family of Noah, but since you are living on this planet, you know that wasn't the case. Things began to go wrong again. Those people who in Noah's time thought "only evil continually" might be gone, but that human disposition didn't die with them. It seems that the writer of Genesis is trying to help us understand just how deep-seated and pervasive our human problem is—this problem we call sin, with its multiple consequences. It's as if the writer were taking us inside the story, almost as if he were trying to make us feel that the problem is so great that even God struggles to cope with it.

But then the good news comes. It's not the end of the story and not the end of the struggle, but it points to where the end will be and reassures us that the eventual consummation will be good. Magnificently good, in fact.

In truth, you wouldn't guess how good it's going to be on the basis of the way it begins. This really big matter starts in the closing verses of the eleventh chapter of Genesis, like this: "Now these are the descendants of Terah" (Genesis 11:27); you see, I *told* you it was an inauspicious beginning. We learn that this long-ago family left their home in Ur of the Chaldeans, a major metropolitan center of its time, to go "into the land of Canaan," and that one of Terah's sons, Abram, was married to a woman named Sarai, who "was barren; she had no child" (Genesis 11:30, 31). We will discover as we work our way through the biblical story that such a statement of apparent hopelessness is the prelude to something special and wonderful, the kind of thing we would label a miracle.

The prospect of a miracle comes a paragraph later, when God asks Abram to leave his security and go into the unknown, with the promise that Abram will "be a blessing," and that in him "all the families of the earth shall be blessed" (Genesis 12:2-3). I submit that the plot for the rest of the biblical story unfolds from just this point.

Mind you, the plot doesn't follow a straight, unerring line; not, at least, from our point of view. But if it did, the story would be quite dull, and as most of us realize, the story of our human race—from a faith point of view—is anything but dull. As we know from the paragraph in which Abram and Sarai were introduced, they were without children. We soon learn that they were already well past the age of childbearing, so the prospect of their offspring becoming "a great nation" is quite absurd (12:2). When at last Isaac, the child of promise, is born, Abram and Sarai—or Abraham and Sarah, as their names have since become—are one hundred years old and ninety years old, respectively.

The intervening years are uneven. At times Abraham and Sarah make some choices that are so hard to defend that the two seem unlikely bearers of the purposes of a holy God. This reminds us that God has no perfect persons with whom to work, so it's necessary to use the best available. That's sometimes where you and I come in.

But it is also true that Abraham and Sarah are quite heroic figures. After all, they leave home and kindred—the secure and the familiar—at an age when those comforts are most important, in order to pursue the call of God. Their contract from God is so lacking in specifics and so general in its promises that this New Testament writer says admiringly that Abraham "set out, not knowing where he was going" (Hebrews 11:8). If Sarah and Abraham sometimes walked erratically on their long journey, I can only marvel that nevertheless they kept going.

And both biblical history and secular history pay Abraham credit. The New Testament sees him as the father of the faithful for both Judaism and Christianity. Hundreds of years later Islam also claimed Abraham as its ancestor via Ishmael, the son born to Abraham through Sarah's maid, Hagar. So it is that students of religion think of Abraham as the father of the three great monotheistic faiths— Judaism, Christianity, and Islam.

Isaac, the son of Sarah and Abraham, seems a rather prosaic figure when compared to his monumental father and Isaac's complex son Jacob. Isaac is most remembered for his nearly being sacrificed by Abraham as a test of faith. Next to his birth, the only other notable moment in Isaac's life was when he was deceived by his younger son Jacob—who positions himself to receive Esau's blessing. But Jacob is another matter. As the writer of Genesis says, Jacob strove with God and with humans and prevailed (Genesis 32:28). If I had done business with Jacob, I would have passed any contract with him before a covey of lawyers; and yet, if I had wanted to talk about things eternal, I would have sought him out, because whatever his failings—and they were several—he had an eye for that which is supremely important.

After Jacob's crucial encounter with God, his name is changed to Israel, a name that is with us still today in what is arguably the most strategic country in the Middle East, and in the inhabitants of that country, the Israelis. Jacob had twelve sons and a daughter by his two wives, the sisters Leah and Rachel, and by two concubines. (See Genesis 35:22b-26.) We speak thereafter of these offspring of Jacob as "the children of Israel" or "the twelve tribes of Israel." The number itself is a kind of tribute to Jacob. When Jesus gathered together his disciples, it is not by chance that he chose twelve. When the writer of Revelation envisions the eternal city, it has twelve gates for the twelve tribes of Israel and twelve foundations for the twelve apostles. (See Revelation 21:12, 14.) The culture of the western world continues to embrace this number, so that we order a dozen of this or that, paying the number twelve the high compliment of a pseudonym, a comfortable nickname so to speak. So it is that Jacob is with us still, each time we buy a carton of eggs or a small box of aspirin.

Most of Jacob's sons are easily forgotten. We think hard to recall Zebulun, Gad, Asher, or Naphtali. But several others more than make up for the lack. Joseph comes center stage in Genesis 37, when the writer begins, "This is the lineage [or story] of Jacob," and continues without pause, "Joseph, seventeen years old, was tending the flock with his brothers."[1] We know that Jacob's story—indeed, the whole family's story—is going to find its plot for some time in this one character, the son named Joseph. Most of the following fourteen chapters—page-wise, nearly a third of the book of Genesis—have Joseph as the lead character.

This is because we have to get the family of Israel into Egypt, and it is Joseph who will be the unwitting instrument of this move. It is in Egypt that the family of Israel will become a nation. Without Egypt this little band of roughly seventy people would quickly intermarry with the peoples around them, and in a generation or two they would not exist as a particular people. But in Egypt, in time, they will be made slaves, so the Egyptians will not marry them, nor will *they* want to marry the Egyptians; and thus the children of Israel

8

will become the *nation* of Israel, a people remaining to this very day, and still as uniquely significant as they ever have been.

But I'm getting ahead of my story—as one must at times, if a story is to be fully told. The other son of Jacob who slips into the plot is Judah. However, as you read the Genesis story you have the feeling that Judah does not so much slip into the plot as intrude upon it. Genesis chapter 37 tells the dramatic story of Joseph being sold into slavery by his brothers, but only after they first contemplate killing him. Chapter 37 ends with the sentence, "Meanwhile the Midianites had sold him [Joseph] in Egypt to Potiphar, one of Pharaoh's officials, the captain of the guard" (Genesis 37:36); and chapter 39 begins, "Now Joseph was taken down to Egypt, and Potiphar, an officer of Pharaoh, the captain of the guard, an Egyptian, bought him from the Ishmaelites who had brought him down there" (Genesis 39:1). Chapter 38 is the Judah interlude.

"It happened at that time," the writer begins in Genesis 38, and proceeds to tell a story that unfolded over a period of at least twenty years. "It happened at that time" is like our storytelling device "Meanwhile, back on the farm"; it reports the events as action that was going on somewhere else, perhaps over an extended period, but running parallel to the story that is temporarily being laid aside. I won't go into the story in detail here, because to do it justice would require at least a chapter all to itself. Chapter 38 tells the beginning of Judah's family line, and it is an unconventional beginning, indeed, just as Judah was an unlikely hero. He was not Jacob's firstborn and heir, nor was he the second, "the spare"; he was not even the third. As the fourth son, Judah had no lineal possibilities. Nevertheless, the first three eliminated themselves, leaving Judah next in line. (See Genesis 49:1-12.)

Nor is Judah's early activity commendable. When Jacob's older sons contemplate killing young Joseph, Judah offers an alternative: "What profit is it if we kill our brother and conceal his blood? Come, let us sell him to the Ishmaelites, and not lay our hands on him, for he is our brother, our own flesh" (Genesis 37:26-27). See Judah, the crafty negotiator: he spares his brother's life but makes some money in the process and still gets rid of him. What Judah doesn't know is that he is keeping the Eternal Plot alive, because by his cleverness he is getting Joseph to Egypt, where Joseph will become one of the most powerful rulers in the land, and where he will pave the way for crucial succeeding chapters in the story.

As the rest of the Genesis story unfolds, and as famine in the land of Canaan forces Jacob's family to seek aid in Egypt, Judah will slowly come into the foreground: first, by becoming the spokesperson for his brothers when making a case with their father (Genesis 43:3, 8); then by pleading for the life of their youngest brother Benjamin before Joseph (Genesis 44:14-34), in one of the longest single speeches in the book of Genesis. The writer of Genesis subtly lets us know what is happening with Judah when he introduces Judah's speech, *"Judah and his brothers* came to Joseph's house" (Genesis 44:14, emphasis added). It is not "the sons of Jacob" or "Joseph's brothers," but "Judah and his brothers." Judah is now a key player in the plot. His significance will be lifted to preeminence when Jacob pronounces his dying blessing on the twelve sons (Genesis 49:8-12).

As I indicated earlier, Joseph's story—which occupies most of the closing section of Genesis—is crucial to the plot line. It is a great story in its own right, so it's not surprising that Nobel Prize–winning German novelist Thomas Mann made four full-length novels from the Joseph story (*Joseph and His Brothers*), as he wound his way through psychological insights. Joseph is no doubt one of the three or four favorite characters for teachers of beginning Sunday school classes, especially for his insistence on doing what is right and his eventual triumph after some very stormy years.

And Joseph gets the last line in the book of Genesis, by way of a burial notice: "And Joseph died, being one hundred ten years old; he was embalmed and placed in a coffin in Egypt" (Genesis 50:26). But before his death, Joseph reminded his brothers that God would "surely" bring them up out of Egypt "to the land that he swore to Abraham, to Isaac, and to Jacob" (Genesis 50:24). Thus Joseph, in a sense the spiritual heir to his father, Jacob, assures his family that they are the inheritors of a divine promise and that they cannot settle down in Egypt; it is only temporary location. This is such an essential point to Joseph that he insists that when the day of exit comes, they will take his bones with them.

Joseph understood well enough that his family had come to Egypt in the purposes of God. I can't say he anticipated the generations of slavery that would follow, but he was altogether certain that the story of his people was not to end in Egypt. Nor did he want—in the instance of his bones—to be left behind. As a participant in a magnificent, God-purposeful story, Joseph wanted to be where the action was going to be.

---

[1] Robert Alter, *The Five Books of Moses* (New York: W. W. Norton & Company, 2004), page 206.

2
The Eternal Plot

Before I go farther into the Bible's remarkable story, I need to interrupt myself to talk about the general background of the Bible. We take it for granted that a book will have a plot. If the plot is hard to find, we wonder if we have missed it through our own inattentiveness or if perhaps the author lost the trail in the process of writing. I say this so I can point out that it's surprising the Bible has a plot. After all, it was written by scores of authors over hundreds of years, and in two different languages, the first portion in Hebrew and the second in Greek. Most of the authors never knew one another, and in a majority of instances they had no idea of what the others wrote. It's hard to imagine scores of authors separated by time and space, living in very different historical periods with experiences unique to their periods coming up with a continuing theme, let alone any really discernible plot.

And to make matters still more complicated, the biblical authors often worked with quite different genres. Genesis reads like a historical novel—a saga, if you please. Leviticus is a law book, Proverbs is a collection of pithy sayings, and Job is a discourse on the injustices of life and how God feels about such injustices. The psalms are exquisite poetry, and the prophets are stern and passionate advocates for righteous living. When you move into the shorter section of the Bible that we call the New Testament, you meet four books that you want to call biographies, except they don't fit the usual structure of a biography. Then we encounter a book called The Acts of the Apostles, which starts out as a history of the early Christian movement but about halfway along becomes primarily the story of one particular leader in the movement, Paul. Then a series of let-

13

ters, most of them written to churches in the ancient Middle East, but some to individuals—and all of them so clearly directed to the original recipients that sometimes you feel as if you're reading other people's mail without their permission, while at the same time sensing that through projection, everything in the letters relates to you. And then the collection ends with an exotic climax that we call The Revelation.

So where's the plot? Or on the other hand, who could ask that a book written under such extraordinary circumstances would have a plot?

The Bible is made up of literally hundreds of stories, each of which easily stands alone. They stand alone so well, in fact, that scores of them have been recited over generations of time, often by people or to people who didn't know that the particular story was part of a larger plot. Adam and Eve, Cain and Abel, the Flood, the Tower of Babel, Daniel in the lions' den, Esther, Job, the story of the good Samaritan, the feeding of the multitudes—the list of familiar stories goes on and on.

And for that matter, those portions of the Bible that are officially classified as poetry, wisdom, or prophetic writings seem often to imply a plot. You can't read, "O Lord, how many are my foes! / Many are rising against me" (Psalm 3:1) without knowing that you have been put right in the middle of someone's wrenching misery. But where's the plot? And what does such a sentence, or any of the short stories I've just mentioned, have to do with some overarching plot?

From the point of view of a literary device, I'm tempted to compare Chaucer's *Canterbury Tales*, or perhaps *The Book of One Thousand and One Nights* (often popularly known as the *Arabian Nights*). But these famous works don't really have a common plot running through their collection. In the first, the individual stories come from the several pilgrims who are on their way to Canterbury; and in the second, the connecting theme is simply the artful way the beautiful Scheherazade manages, by her storytelling (with such now-familiar characters as Aladdin, Sinbad the Sailor, and Ali Baba), to divert King Shahryar from his planned vengeful murders.

But the stories in the Bible are not simply hung together by some artificial device, however artistic that might be. Each has its own connection with the grand plot, usually quite directly, and sometimes by inference. And the better the reader knows the plot, the more fascinating it is to see the connections and to marvel, at times, at the intricacy with which the pieces come together.

And what is this plot? It is the story of God's relationship with our human race. In its own way it is a love story—the strangest, most robust and most challenging love story one can imagine. The Old Testament unfolds this love story especially through the relationship of God with the people of Israel, while in the New Testament the plot turns to God and the church; but in each instance, it is the story of divine love putting up with the indifference and even the rebelliousness of the beloved.

The plot is made still more complicated by the fact that although God's love is directed especially toward Israel and the church, the ultimate object of this love is our entire human race. Thus the Bible verse that so many of us memorized in our earliest Sunday-school days: "For God so loved the *world* ..." (John 3:16, emphasis added). Israel and the church are not meant to be the end of God's love, but the means to a greater end—the entire human race.

But our human story can never be told simply through institutions and nations and movements. Ralph Waldo Emerson said, "There is properly no history; only biography." So to tell the story of Israel is to tell the story of Abraham, Isaac, and Jacob; of Moses and Joshua and Deborah and Jael. And to tell the story of the church is to speak of several Marys, of Peter and Paul, of Lydia and Cornelius. Israel may go astray as a nation, but it will do so with the help, in one instance, of Aaron, and in another, of Gideon, or of Ahab and Jezebel; and to tell the story of the church is not to tell simply the decisions made at a council in Jerusalem, but to speak of Stephen's sermon, of Mary's readiness to make her home a meeting place for the worshipers, and of Paul and Barnabas at first working together wonderfully, then separating fitfully. All of this is the story of the people of God, whether Israel or the church—but it happens through the lives of individuals.

So this story of God's relationship to our human race is at once the story of the special people of God, through whom God would become manifest to the human race, and of those persons to whom

15

the witness is made. Abel is part of the story, who "through his faith ... still speaks" today (Hebrews 11:4); but his brother Cain, the murderer, is also part of our human story and part of the biblical story, because this biblical story is the record of the constant conflict between good and evil. Moses is part of the plot, as the one who leads God's people out of the bondage of Egypt, and Pharaoh is part of the story as one who tries to prevent their exodus. And as the plot unfolds in the pages of scripture we sense that it is at work still in our lives, our times, our circumstances, and our decisions. And the better we understand the scripture plot, the readier we are to contribute to the redemption of our planet through our own participation in the eternal plot.

Thus, as we read the Scriptures it is our privilege—indeed, our calling—to find our place in the story. Herein is a peculiar and dramatic difference in reading the Bible. Those who read the Book in faith become part of the plot. When I read secular history, I may well be moved by it, be grateful for its finest personalities, and even be inspired to be a better citizen of my country and of the world. But as I read the scriptures, a deeper, more existential thing happens: I enter into the plot. I do not simply empathize with the biblical stories, I enlist myself as a continuing contributor. This is the point the author of the New Testament book of Hebrews makes. Having listed for us the faith-heroes of centuries past, he draws us into the story as their successors: "Yet all these, though they were commended for their faith, did not receive what was promised, since God had provided something better so that they would not, apart from us, be made perfect" (Hebrews 11:39-40).

I mentioned earlier that the Bible was written by dozens of authors; the truth is, we can't easily estimate how many. Some authors—like Jeremiah, Ezra, and Nehemiah in the Old Testament, and Paul in the New—identify themselves, but in many instances no such identification is made, and the name by which the book is known is one that was added later, by tradition. Scholars have developed their own sophisticated way of calculating who the author might be for a given book—as with the Chronicles, for example—but what one scholar proves, some later scholar usually wants to improve on.

But the several authors, known and unknown, always speak on

God's behalf. Often they declare themselves in so many words: "Thus saith the Lord." In other instances they leave the matter to be inferred, but the very style of their utterance indicates clearly that they see themselves not as independent spiritual entrepreneurs, but as persons entrusted with a message from God. They take this position without arrogance and without bothering to prove their point. We commonly say that the Bible is inspired by God—specifically by the Holy Spirit—but of course persons may have quite different ideas in mind when they speak of divine inspiration. Personally, I believe that the Bible is uniquely inspired: that it is different from any other book and that it is a gift from God. But I believe that this inspiration was played out through human instruments. Thus one can see the fingerprints of the various human authors; in some instances, one might even refer to those fingerprints as smudges, because the humanness of the authors is altogether clear. Nevertheless, these human touches do not in any way diminish the divine source.

When we try to discern how the books of the Bible came together in their present form, we have few clues to work with. This is especially true of the books of the Hebrew Scriptures, which we Christians usually refer to as the Old Testament. According to one popular Jewish tradition, the canon of these books was established at the time of Ezra and Nehemiah, in the fifth and sixth centuries B.C. There is logic to support the tradition: the people of Israel were seeking to reestablish themselves in their homeland following their Babylonian and Persian exile, and Ezra and Nehemiah worked earnestly to bring the nation back to its sacred roots. What could be more important at such a time than to affirm or reaffirm in a formal way the writings that formed the foundation of their faith and their personhood? Others argue that the final collection of books that we know as the Old Testament wasn't settled until perhaps A.D. 90 or 100. Again, logic makes an argument, because after the destruction of the Temple in A.D. 70, Israel's religious leaders must have put forth extraordinary effort to hold their people together even as they were being physically dispersed.

I think it's a bit easier to imagine how the twenty-seven books of the New Testament came together. I like to call it the democracy of the Holy Spirit. Let me explain what I mean. We know that a body of literature developed very early in the history of the Christian church. The apostle Paul, in particular, wrote numerous letters not only to congregations he had founded but also to some (like Rome, for instance) that he hoped to someday visit. We have no idea how many letters Paul wrote beyond those in our New Testament canon, nor how many other letters were written by other apostles and early leaders in the church.

And then there were the Gospels. We have four, Matthew, Mark, Luke, and John. As Luke explains as he begins his Gospel, "Since many have undertaken to set down an orderly account of the events that have been fulfilled among us," he has decided himself "to write an orderly account" (Luke 1:1, 3). But how many are the "many" to whom Luke refers, and who were they? We can easily imagine some persons who might have ventured either to record their own memories of Jesus or to tell their memories to someone else who had the ability to write.

How is it, then, that from the many stories of Jesus that were written even by the time Luke's Gospel was in use—and the unnumbered letters that Paul and others might have written—we now have those books that constitute our New Testament? It is often assumed that these books were authorized by the Catholic Church. In truth, this is after the fact. The Second Trullan Council in A.D. 692 included a statement of the books in the New Testament, but in doing so the Council was only formalizing information already contained in a number of documents by Athanasius, Jerome, and Augustine in the late fourth and early fifth centuries; and these in turn reflected what had been going on in the church for several centuries. Indeed, records from a wide variety of places indicate that by the middle of the second century nearly all the books making up the New Testament constituted a kind of informal canon in the use of the churches scattered abroad; and the four Gospels and the Epistles of Paul were accepted by the end of the first century.[1] In other words, the church was barely entering its second generation when the basic body of the New Testament was generally established and accepted.

This brings me back to the phrase I used earlier—the democracy of the Holy Spirit. Our generation, with computers and immediate reproduction and transmission of material, can hardly imagine a world where writing materials were precious and the recording of material was tedious and time consuming. Suppose, therefore, that you are part of a late-first-century congregation of believers who have just received a letter from Paul, or perhaps a book of good news, the story of Jesus. You feel the wonder of this document; for you, it is a gift from God—and therefore something you want to share with a friend in a congregation elsewhere.

You can do so only with hundreds of hours of careful copying—on papyrus if you are fortunate, but more likely on the hide of an animal. You will go to such lengths only if you believe passionately in the value of these books. And suppose, too, that at rather frequent intervals the people who read or circulate these books are subject to arrest, imprisonment, and even violent death, so that possessing one or more of these books may put one's life in danger. One must believe in these books—and the faith they teach—with a life-and-death earnestness.

So how is it that of the many stories of Jesus that were written already in Luke's time, and of the scores if not hundreds of epistles or letters, that these books—twenty-seven of them, finally—became our New Testament? Quite simply, because their first readers found in them something so eternally valuable that they would (at the least) laboriously and tediously make copies to pass on to friends and to other churches; and (at the most) give their lives to protect these books and to circulate them. I call this the democracy of the Holy Spirit, meaning that these books survived not because some organization endorsed them, but because tens of thousands of ordinary and extraordinary believers read them, loved them, copied them, and passed them on; and I believe that it was the Holy Spirit in these believers that recognized the inspiration of the Holy Spirit in these books.

I submit that we are looking at two miracles. First, there is the miracle of inspiration. As I said earlier, I see the Scriptures as uniquely inspired by God. This is quite an astonishing miracle in light of the variety of authors and the circumstances of writing, and the period of time in which the collection of books came into existence—especially in the case of what we call the Old Testament.

The second miracle is the Bible's preservation. The Hebrew

Scriptures were entrusted to a relatively minor country; not a mover and shaker in the fashion of Egypt, Babylon, Persia, or Greece, but a nation that much of the time was subject to some other national power; and a people who were sometimes carried captive by those other powers. And since those other ancient peoples had gods of their own, they were ready enough to obliterate the religious teachings of Israel, especially since many of those teachings seemed quite absurd to others. Nor did the Jews (the name by which Israel came eventually to be known) have secure libraries in which they could keep their sacred books. The memorable libraries of the pre-Christian era were in such cities as Alexandria, Pergamum, or Athens; not in Jerusalem.

The same issue of preservation was, if anything, even more pronounced in the story of the New Testament. For the first three centuries of Christian history, the church suffered frequent periods of persecution. It was not yet the institution of later times, with schools, libraries, and often the benefit of public and political favor. On the contrary, to be a Christian was often to put one's career and life in peril, and to shelter the church's writings was to incriminate one's self. And yet this people not only kept the church's writings from destruction but also made copies in astonishing abundance.

Here's a measure of the abundance: well over five thousand New Testament Greek manuscripts are in existence today—portions or entire copies of New Testament books. Many of these manuscripts date from the third century, some from the second, and one from either late in the first century or very early in the second. In addition to these Greek manuscripts, we have thousands of portions of ancient translations of the New Testament in Latin, Ethiopic, Slavic, and Armenian—totaling some 24,000.

We can begin to appreciate the significance of these figures when we compare other ancient writings. Tacitus, the premier Roman historian, wrote his classic work around A.D. 116 (a generation or more after the New Testament books), but only one manuscript of a portion of his work dates as far back as A.D. 850, and the next oldest portion dates from the eleventh century. Or take Julius Caesar's *Commentarii de Bello Gallico* (*Commentaries on the Gallic War*), written between 58 and 50 B.C—material you would expect to be preserved since it was written by the great emperor and general. Yet very few copies remain, and the oldest of these is from 900 years after the original was written.

How remarkable, indeed, that writings about a young Jewish teacher who was in the public eye for barely three years—and in a relatively obscure part of the great Roman Empire—should be preserved in such vast numbers. This fact alone reveals how the works of scholars and personalities apparently far more important in their time pale in comparison! And especially, if I may repeat, when the people who were copying and circulating these writings were rarely in public favor and often were preserving these books while in danger of their lives.

From time to time, books appear—sometimes as fiction and sometimes as works of quasi-scholarship—that build upon a fanciful conspiracy theory suggesting that an ancient document has been suppressed by some religious or political power, and that these writings, if fully known, would destroy the Christian story. In doing so, such books—knowingly or not—are turning the Christian story in upon itself. It is not quite a conspiracy story, of course, because the enemies of Christianity were rarely, if ever, organized in any hidden way; they didn't need to be organized, since the power of the state was generally on their side. But Christianity survived and grew because, as someone has said, the Christians outlived, out-loved, out-thought, and out-died their opposition. And with such extraordinary living, loving, thinking, and dying, they preserved the book that continues today to capture the minds and souls of untold millions.

A miracle, indeed. A miracle both in the book's inspiration and in its remarkable preservation. A miracle we can purchase at will, and read or lay aside at our convenience. But a miracle that, for all its commonness, still transforms those readers who approach it with ready hearts and minds.

---

[1] David Ewert, *A General Introduction to the Bible* (Grand Rapids: Academic Books; Zondervan Publishing House, 1983), page 129.

21

3

From Exit to Entrance

Exodus Through Deuteronomy

W HEN I INTERRUPTED OUR STORY A CHAPTER AGO, JOSEPH, AS HE LAY
dying, was telling the family of Israel that they must someday carry
his bones out of the land of Egypt. Why? Because Israel's future was
not in Egypt, but in "the land that [God] swore to Abraham, to Isaac,
and to Jacob" (Genesis 50:24).

At the time of Joseph's death, I suppose it would have been easy
for the Israelites to settle into the area of Egypt that Pharaoh had
assigned to them. The land was good, their future seemed secure,
and they were favored as the family of Egypt's second-in-command.
But when the book of Exodus opens nearly four hundred years later,
the scene has changed dramatically. The Israelites, "fruitful and pro-
lific," have grown from a family of fewer than a hundred persons, so
that now, "the land was filled with them" (Exodus 1:7). And with the
passing of time, Egypt's new leaders have forgotten Joseph and his
great service to their nation, so that now the Israelites are seen as a
potential enemy rather than the sheepherding kin of a beloved
leader.

So the Egyptian government "oppress[ed] them with forced
labor"—that is, they made the Israelites into a population of slaves—
and "were ruthless in all the tasks that they imposed on them"
(Exodus 1:11, 14). When the Israelites continued to multiply, the
king of Egypt ordered the midwives to kill any newborn, Hebrew boy
babies. When this strategy failed, the king decreed that every boy
born to the Hebrews should be thrown into the Nile. (See Exodus
1:22.)

It is here that our plot takes another significant turn. As I said in
chapter 1, it was crucial to get the family of Israel to Egypt, because

23

it was through the experience of slavery and exclusion that they became a nation. But the time comes when they must be freed if they are to fulfill their divine purposes. So it is that a husband and wife from the tribe of Levi—who, at this point, are left anonymous— dare to defy the king's decree and save their newborn, baby boy. But after three months, the couple can hide him no longer. So the mother puts the child into the Nile River as commanded, in a papyrus basket—a kind of miniature ark—and the baby's older sister watches the infant from a distance. (See Exodus 2:1-4.)

Well, some of you know the next part of the story. The daughter of Pharaoh (of all people!) sees the tiny basket, has it brought to her, and takes pity on the crying child. Through the baby's older sister, the infant's own mother is enlisted to nurse the child. Eventually Pharaoh's daughter names the child Moses, "Because," she said, "I drew him out of the water" (Exodus 2:10). Thus the child is named for the very agent that was supposed to destroy him. It is a kind of parable-in-action: God uses the playbook of the enemy as the instrument of grace.

The Old Testament portion of the Eternal Plot has literally hundreds of characters, but if you want to identify some of the towering figures, think of Moses along with Abraham, the beginning of the faith-line, and King David, who becomes symbolic of the messianic king. But Moses' story isn't simple nor his pathway unerring. He is trained in the courts of Egypt, but at the age of forty he fumbles tragically in his first attempt to help his people, Israel. He then spends the next forty years of his life in obscurity, as a fugitive from justice and a backcountry shepherd.

But at age eighty, Moses becomes the hero who, through a series of plagues and confrontations, breaks Pharaoh's hold on the people of Israel, leading the ragtag body of slaves into freedom. Where Genesis gets its name as the book of beginnings, Exodus takes its name as the story of an exit—from a philosophical point of view, perhaps the greatest exit history has ever known. No wonder, on the one hand, that America's slave population took Moses' story as their template of political freedom ("Go down, Moses, / Way down in Egypt-land. / Tell ol' Pharaoh, / Let my people go"); and on another hand, generations of Christian preachers and teachers have used the same story to describe spiritual freedom (we leave the slavery of sin in order to go to the promised land, Canaan).

But although the book of Exodus gets its name from this grand march to freedom, more than half of its pages are spent in the giving of the Law (the Ten Commandments and elements surrounding these key concepts) and the plans for Israel's first place of worship. I submit that civilization cannot long survive without these two components: law—because even the best of persons need guidance as to right and wrong, or else order will turn into chaos; and a place to worship—because unless humanity has some sense of God to exalt the meaning of life, we will find ways to avoid and pervert even the best of laws.

Leviticus

And speaking of laws, we are ready to enter the book of Leviticus. This book gets its name from the tribe of Levi—the tribe from which Moses himself came, as I mentioned earlier. You've probably been told that the book of Leviticus is tedious. Someone may even have confided that they wonder why it is included in the Bible. Well, believe me, it has its place in the plot.

But before I go further, let me tell you something about the tribe of Levi. At one of the crucial junctures in the book of Exodus, at a time when it appeared that the nation had abandoned God—and worse, that they had done so under the leadership of Aaron, Moses' brother and confidante—Moses threw out a challenge to the nation: "Who is on the LORD's side? Come to me!" Immediately, "the sons of Levi gathered around him" (Exodus 32:26). From that time forward, the Levites were set aside as the priestly tribe.

In practice, they were much more than simply the religious leaders. They provided the music for worship. They were also the caretakers of the place of worship; when the place of worship was a portable tabernacle, they were the porters who took the building down, carried it to the next place, and reassembled it. We might well think of them, therefore, as the church staff in a modern congregation.

But again, the Levites were much more. They taught the law of

A HOP, SKIP, AND A JUMP THROUGH THE BIBLE

God to the people; call them, then, Israel's teachers. They also interpreted the law; call them lawyers—theologian-lawyers, because the only law the people had was the law of God, so that to interpret the law was to enunciate the will of God. When certain crucial health issues arose—particularly those related to the most dreaded disease of the time, usually referred to as leprosy—it was the Levites who examined the afflicted and determined the seriousness of the illness. So, call the Levites, if not doctors, then medical counselors.

In total, we might refer to the Levites as the nation's clergy, musicians, teachers, temple attendants, lawyers, and doctors; in a sense, the nation's professionals. The rest of Israel were farmers and herdsmen. The Levites had no land of their own, but they were assigned forty-eight cities among the other tribes. The other tribes supported the Levites by their tithes, their offerings of a portion of their goods or income.

Now, let me be honest with you. The book of Leviticus is an acquired taste. It may take you a while to appreciate its meticulous attention to detail, its careful lists of clean and unclean animals, its prescriptions for ritual cleanliness, and its concern for ritual and moral holiness. A great many years ago a teacher of mine referred to Leviticus as "the book of sacred *etiquette*." That's an appropriate word. You will appreciate what this book is all about if you will listen for two phrases that appear and re-appear like a symphonic theme: "I am the LORD your God," and "You shall be holy, for I the LORD your God am holy."

But let's face it. Our contemporary culture isn't much given to etiquette; a great many seem to feel that the fewer the rules, the better. But ponder this. When the theological experts of Jesus' day asked him to identify the great commandment, the one that was "the first of all," Jesus replied, "The first is, 'Hear, O Israel: the Lord our God, the Lord is one; you shall love the Lord your God with all your heart, and with all your soul, and with all your mind, and with all your strength.' The second is this, 'You shall love your neighbor as yourself.' There is no other commandment greater than these" (Mark 12:28-31). When Jesus gave the second half of the great commandment, he was quoting the book of Leviticus—specifically, Leviticus 19:18.

B. C + C E!

All this to say: the plot line may seem lost in details in the book of Leviticus, but it is as significant as ever. Remember the plot? God's relationship to our human race. And what is Leviticus all about? Maintaining that relationship through sacred rituals and a profound concern for any matter of conduct that might imperil it. And how, especially, is this relationship lived out in the routine of daily life? By loving our neighbor, and by showing that love in such down-to-earth matters as: "You shall rise before the aged, and defer to the old ... you shall not oppress the alien ... you shall not cheat in measuring length, weight, or quantity" (Leviticus 19:32-33, 35).

There's nothing boring about that. It's as real as a friend in a home for the aging, the treatment of the migrant worker, and the laws of the marketplace. Sacred etiquette, before God and before our neighbor.

Numbers

The book of Numbers gets its name from the census of Israel, which was implemented as the nation made its way through the wilderness, from Egypt to the land of promise. Such a numbering was essential if this new nation—this body of people just out of slavery, with no heritage of self-government—was to become an organized, viable people.

But this name, Numbers, which was first given to the book in the Septuagint (the translation of the Old Testament into the Greek that was begun around 250 B.C.) is far too prosaic for the far-ranging content of the book. The Hebrew title of the book, "In the Wilderness," which is taken from the first common noun in the book of Numbers, describes where the action takes place; and all things considered, it is also a pretty good philosophical summary of the events recorded in the book.

Because in Numbers, the people of Israel get close enough to their destination, Canaan, their cherished land of promise, to send out a committee of twelve (one from each tribe) to look over the land. These spies bring back pomegranates and figs, and "a single cluster of grapes" of such abundance that "they carried it on a pole between two of them" (Numbers 13:23). I'm fascinated that the logo

27

of modern Israel's tourist bureau depicts this scene: two men carrying a bunch of grapes on a pole between them.

But beyond their agreement on the abundance of the land, the committee of twelve split by a vote of ten to two. Ten men (it was an all-male committee) described it as "a land that devours its inhabitants; and all the people that we saw in it are of great size" (Numbers 13:32)—a remarkably contradictory statement!—while the minority, Caleb and Joshua, insisted, "Let us go up at once and occupy it, for we are well able to overcome it" (Numbers 13:30). Of course the people went with the majority report—not simply because it was a majority, but because it is always easier to go with inaction than with challenge. God's judgment was that Israel would wander in the wilderness for forty years—one year for each day the scouts had spent in their investigation—time enough, that is, for the adult generation to die off. But of course the nation didn't need a divine judgment to postpone their entry into the promised land for forty years; their self-doubts—and worse, their doubts of God—were enough to close the door to the future. This basic format has been repeated thousands of times in human history: sometimes in the lives of nations, more often in corporations and institutions (including churches), and daily in the lives of individuals.

Both history and legend have made Moses a decidedly larger-than-life figure, but his contemporaries didn't always see him that way. It wasn't simply that some primitive polling organization reported from their sampling that people were unhappy with Moses' administration. Much worse, Moses' own siblings, Aaron and Miriam, spoke against him, not for failures of leadership, but because he was married to a Cushite woman (Numbers 12). It was a case of racial or ethnic prejudice, and as with many instances of prejudice, other elements of jealousy no doubt were involved.

Not long after, a Levite and several members of the tribe of Reuben brought together two hundred and fifty men—"leaders of the congregation ... well-known men"—in what appears on the surface to have been a populist movement. "All the congregation are holy," they said, "every one of them, and the LORD is among them. So why then do you exalt yourselves above the assembly of the LORD?" (Numbers 16:2-3).

28

FROM EXIT TO ENTRANCE

I have a feeling that the pressures of leadership wore on Moses. So one day when the people were calling for water, Moses did to himself what no enemy could have done: he shut himself out of the crowning hour of his leadership. Instructed by God to speak to a rock to give forth water, Moses chose instead to strike the rock—twice, in fact. Because of his act of disobedient arrogance, Moses was forbidden to enter the land he would lead the people toward for forty years (see Numbers 20:1-13).

As you can see, there's a rather dark, heavy quality in much of the book of Numbers. But there are several chapters of comic relief in the story of Balak and Balaam, and Balaam's donkey. If you allow yourself to enjoy the humor of the story, you realize that King Balak and the royal counselor, Balaam, show themselves more the fools than does the oft-maligned donkey. Indeed, the donkey is the hero of the story, and the two pompous figures—the one a king and the other an intellectual religionist—show themselves to be the bumblers. I wonder if anyone has ever thought of making this story into a comic opera?

Before Numbers ends, we are introduced to Joshua, Moses' ultimate successor (see Numbers 27:12-23), and we see an interesting legal provision for women regarding their right in choosing whom they will marry (see Numbers 36). It isn't everything, but it's a significant step in the right direction—as much, I suspect, as society was ready to receive at the time.

And whatever else you remember or forget from Numbers, remind yourself that this book has preserved for us one of the loveliest benedictions the human race can know:

The LORD bless you and keep you;
the LORD make his face to shine upon you, and be gracious to you;
the LORD lift up his countenance upon you, and give you peace.
(Numbers 6:24-26)

But we are getting near the promised land, so we must get on with the plot.

Deuteronomy

Deuteronomy, the last book of the section of the Old Testament we often refer to as the Pentateuch and which Jews identify as the

29

Torah, gets its name from two Greek words, meaning "second law." I like to think of it as Moses' valedictory address. "These are the words," the book begins, "that Moses spoke to all Israel beyond the Jordan" (Deuteronomy 1:1).

The ultimate business of the book is summarized in God's counsel to the people via Moses: "See, I have set the land before you; go in and take possession of the land that I swore to your ancestors, to Abraham, to Isaac, and to Jacob, to give to them and to their descendants after them" (Deuteronomy 1:8). The people are now on the edge of the land that had been promised to their ancestors centuries before. It is important for them to remember that what they have is not their invention, so to speak, but their inheritance.

This sense of history pervades the Old Testament, and the New Testament picks up the same theme by establishing—in the very beginning of the Gospel of Matthew—the tie of the new with the old.

Broadly speaking, the book of Deuteronomy tells its story in two forms, by recounting God's wondrous acts on behalf of Israel, and by re-enunciating the Law of the Lord, which is the unique possession of Israel. The recounting of God's acts is also, of course, a record of Israel's frequent waywardness. We think of grace as a New Testament theme, but the concept shows itself in every detail of God's relationship with the fledgling nation that is now about to claim its promise.

Moses makes it brutally clear that it is by no merit of their own that Israel has been chosen, and he appeals in the most vigorous language for the people to remember this. Moses warns them that they will be in danger, when they find themselves prosperous in their new home, should they forget the God who brought them there. And they will be in danger, too, of forgetting the kind of character God expects of them: they worship a God "who is not partial and takes no bribe, who executes justice for the orphan and the widow, and who loves the strangers, providing them food and clothing." Such a God requires a godly people: "You shall also love the stranger, for you were strangers in the land of Egypt" (Deuteronomy 10:17-19).

Later, Moses lays out fearful alternatives: if the nation walks with God, they will be blessed; if they disobey the laws and thus the covenant that binds them to God, they will be cursed. Moses' appeal is vigorous and compelling. Scholars ponder, of course, whether these words were actually spoken by Moses or if they were compiled later by priestly writers. But this much is obvious, the words and the style in which they are spoken have the sound of someone who is speaking to a people whom he loves fiercely, and to whom he feels he is delivering his last spiritual will and testament.

As Deuteronomy ends, Moses ascends Mount Nebo to a high place opposite Jericho, where the Lord shows him "the whole land: Gilead as far as Dan.... 'This is the land of which I swore to Abraham, to Isaac, and to Jacob, saying, "I will give it to your descendants"; I have let you see it with your eyes, but you shall not cross over there'" (Deuteronomy 34:1, 4). And there the great liberator and lawgiver, Moses, died, with his sight unimpaired and his vigor unabated. He had led the people in exiting, and he was leaving them now at the place of entrance. But how would they do without him?

4

A Flag Is Born

From Joshua to David

JOSHUA HAD KNOWN FOR SOME TIME THAT HE WOULD EVENTUALLY succeed Moses. But there's never enough lead-time for a job like the one Joshua was facing. How do you succeed a legend? You can remind yourself, of course, that the people sometimes wanted to rebel against Moses, but while this may remind you that even legends have their troubles, it isn't very reassuring.

So we are glad that the book of Joshua opens as it does, with God saying to Joshua, "My servant Moses is dead. Now proceed to cross the Jordan, you and all this people, into the land that I am giving to them" (Joshua 1:2). And we're not surprised that part of Joshua's commissioning is a command that he shall not turn "to the right hand or to the left" from the law of God that had been given to Moses. If Joshua follows this counsel, he need not be "frightened or dismayed, for the LORD your God is with you wherever you go" (Joshua 1:7, 9).

Remember how, forty years earlier, twelve spies went into the land of promise and returned with a report that postponed the program for a generation? Now Joshua sends out spies, but only two of them; and they see themselves as an action team, not as a consultative committee. (See Joshua 2.)

Where do spies take up residence when they are planning the invasion of a secure city? These two spies went to the house of a prostitute, Rahab. I suspect you could write a novel about why they chose this house, speculating for three hundred pages about all the conflicting aspects in their decision. One thing is sure: Rahab was a remarkable woman. Had her trade made her a student of character? Or had she become so accustomed to living on the edge of the law

33

that she was willing to take risks in ways more respected citizens would not?

Or was she one of those God-seekers who, quite beyond logic, have a hunger for God that guides their decisions? Rahab hid the spies because, she said, "I know that the LORD has given [Israel] the land" (Joshua 2:9). So it was that Israel not only conquered Jericho, but Rahab married into the nation and became—as we shall see when we get to the New Testament—an ancestor of Jesus Christ (Matthew 1:5).

The remainder of the book of Joshua is pretty much made up of military activity, with an unseemly amount of destruction and bloodshed. Now let me be honest with you. As far as my own tastes are concerned, I don't really like this book. I am decidedly uncomfortable with the orders to wipe out entire cities. But you see, the Bible is not a feel-good book, it is an *honest* book. It tells us what life is like, not what we wish it were. It constantly challenges us to make life what it should be, but it never suggests that these goals will be easy to achieve or that they will be without serious costs.

Hundreds of years earlier, Abraham, Israel's revered father, had been told that his descendants would be slaves for generations, until it was time for them to claim their inheritance; but the time was not yet, because "the iniquity of the Amorites is not yet complete" (Genesis 15:16). The Bible shows our planet as a place that cannot forever endure evil; the land itself will "[vomit] out its inhabitants" (Leviticus 18:25). I offer no explanation, only a question or two: when we humans engage in the tragic bloodletting of war, is it an instance of judgment in which we are sometimes the agents and sometimes the recipients? And when cropland becomes sterile through our greed or ugly by our concrete, is the land vomiting its inhabitants? Don't blame God for such judgments. Consider rather that when we sow the wind, we reap the whirlwind (Hosea 8:7).

Judges

Transitions are tricky and dangerous. The transition that took place between Moses and Joshua was almost seamless. The same cannot be said, unfortunately, for what followed Joshua's reign.

The writer of the book of Judges puts it succinctly: "The people worshiped the LORD all the days of Joshua, and all the days of the elders who outlived Joshua, who had seen all the great work that the LORD had done for Israel. . . . Then the Israelites did what was evil in the sight of the LORD and worshiped the Baals; and they abandoned the LORD, the God of their ancestors, who had brought them out of the land of Egypt" (Judges 2:7, 11-12). There's a cycle in the book of Judges. It runs like this: Israel prospers, they forget God, they follow other gods, their enemies overwhelm them, they cry out for help, God sends a redeeming judge, they again have peace and prosperity. And there the cycle begins again. If anything about this cycle looks familiar to you, I'm not surprised. Most of us have known something of this cycle in our own walk with God.

But if you like adventure, Judges is a fun read. A teacher in my youth called Judges "The Story of Israel's Wild West Days." He drew his title from the closing verse in the book, a verse the original author apparently intended as a summary of the story he had just told: "In those days there was no king in Israel; all the people did what was right in their own eyes" (Judges 21:25). It was a culture where people took the law into their own hands. It's exciting to read about, but one where it would have been dangerous to live.

Those who led Israel between Joshua and King Saul were referred to as "judges," thus the title of this seventh book of the Old Testament. They were part-time leaders, whose basic role really was to settle disputes—probably much the way a small-claims court judge would do in our day. But since they were the only symbols of authority, the judges became the leaders the people gathered around at times when Israel fought invading powers.

And because of the nature of the times, these leaders were often dramatic and unforgettable characters. Take Deborah, the prophetess who was also a judge. When she called upon Barak to lead Israel against their oppressors, he answered, "If you will go with me, I will go; but if you will not go with me, I will not go" (Judges 4:8). They went to battle together and with the help of an unlikely homemaker, Jael, won a great victory, then sang a memorable duet. You'll find it in Judges 5.

Of course one can't read this book without marveling at Gideon.

Most people know his name from the remarkable ministry of putting Bibles in hotel rooms, and have no idea about the biblical character behind the name. When God called Gideon, the nervous farmer insisted he wasn't qualified, and unfortunately he lived up to his own evaluation in the end. But in the meantime, he gave Israel some of her better days. (See Judges 6–8.)

And of course no one can forget Samson. He was a one-man wrecking crew, hardly the stuff a national leader would be made of. But somehow his physical exploits energized his people—perhaps much the way a small nation today glories in an Olympic gold medal. Of course Samson's moral lapses were as memorable as his athletic victories, and in his spectacular death he conquered more than in all his life. (See Judges 13–16.)

With all its violence and repeated spiritual failures, the book of Judges impresses us most for the simple fact of Israel's survival: the surrounding nations were better organized and had far more military resources. If the book of Judges were all we knew of Israel, we would expect them to have gone the way of the Hittites and the Perizzites, lost in obscurity. One wouldn't guess that a nation led at times by Ehud, Shamgar, Tola, and Jair would be the center of the Eternal Plot, still in dramatic existence in the twenty-first century.

Ruth

The book of Ruth is popularly known as one of the greatest love stories ever written. One of my long-ago teachers called it "God's silver lining to the book of Judges." Both phrases fit. There's no doubt that the book of Judges needs a silver lining, but Ruth doesn't hold much promise when its second line reads, "there was a famine in the land" (Ruth 1:1).

The famine is so bad, in fact, that "a certain man of Bethlehem," Elimelech, takes his wife and two sons to Moab. Hebrews just didn't do that sort of thing. Because of an ancient enmity, a Moabite was not to be welcomed into Israel "even to the tenth generation" (Deuteronomy 23:3-4), so of course no Israelite would easily move to Moab, even in a time of trouble.

Once there, matters got worse. Elimelech died and his two sons marry Moabite girls— unthinkable! Then, the two sons died, and we are left with a widow, Naomi, and her two widowed daughters-in-law, Orpah and Ruth. But if you're a faithful reader of the Bible you know that circumstances like this are simply the Bible's way of saying, "Now we've got trouble in just the place we want it!"—that is, where miracles can begin to happen.

From a romantic perspective (a love story, you know), the daughter-in-law Ruth pledges unwavering loyalty to her mother-in-law, Naomi, out of which comes an unlikely romance with an older man, Boaz, who just happens to have a kinship responsibility to Ruth's deceased husband and who also happens to fall in love with Ruth. (See Ruth 1–4.)

But the best part of the story is still to come, and it comes in a genealogy after all the action—almost as if a movie were to hold its denouement until the last, smallest lines of the credit listings. We learn that the child born to Ruth and Boaz is an ancestor to David, Israel's legendary king (Ruth 4:13-22).

And there's more, much more. When we get to the New Testament, we find that this descendant of Boaz and Ruth is part of the ancestral line of our Lord Jesus Christ (Matthew 1:5-6).

You see? The Eternal Plot is steadily developing, even in the erratic era of the judges. And yes, the book of Ruth is indeed a love story—the story of God's love for our human race, as eventually unfolded at Calvary.

First Samuel

I wish I could tell stories the way the Bible does. When some unknown author begins, "There was a certain man of Ramathaim, a Zuphite from the hill country of Ephraim" (1 Samuel 1:1), we have no idea what is in store for us. It all sounds so prosaic, but we are being led into the story of one of Israel's towering figures, Samuel. Indeed, I'll dare to call him one of history's towering figures, because Samuel is one of those persons who is significant not only in his own right, but also in the people he brings into the path of history.

Samuel was one of the Bible's miracle babies, born to parents when natural circumstances said that a birth was impossible (see 1 Samuel 1–2:11). While still a boy, he was entrusted by God with a message for his aged mentor, Eli (see 1 Samuel 3). In time Samuel became a judge in Israel. In many ways he was the most notable of Israel's judges in that he was also their spiritual leader. Ironically, however, though Samuel's sons succeeded him politically, they didn't possess the same spiritual qualities: "They took bribes and perverted justice" (1 Samuel 8:3).

So Israel asked for a king. This was more than an expression of disappointment in Samuel's sons; it was a call for an entirely different kind of government. The people wanted this, they said, "that we also may be like other nations" (1 Samuel 8:20). They could hardly have said a more revolutionary thing. Israel had been called to be a *holy* people, and to be *holy* in a biblical sense is to be different than the surrounding culture. Israel was doing nothing other than denying its very reason for existence.

But as the Bible describes the divine nature, God has an endless capacity for accommodation and has been working since Eden with the stuff we humans provide, whether good, bad, or indifferent. God therefore counseled Samuel to give them what they want, but warn them of the consequences. Israel, being human, wasn't worried about the consequences.

They got a person of great promise, Saul, of the tribe of Benjamin. "There was not a man among the people of Israel more handsome than he; he stood head and shoulders above everyone else" (1 Samuel 9:2). It isn't hard to imagine the way our contemporary political pundits would describe Saul. And as it happens, he was every bit as good as his appearances. When it was time for his enthronement, he hid himself "among the baggage" (1 Samuel 10:22). When "some worthless fellows" scorned him, "he held his peace" (1 Samuel 10:27). At that time there was no palace, but Saul didn't need one; he continued operating his farm. After his first great victory, his supporters wanted to execute those who had belittled him. Saul answered, "No one shall be put to death this day, for today the LORD has brought deliverance to Israel" (1 Samuel 11:13).

But power, and the adulation that comes with it, is intoxicating. Saul began taking powers to himself that belonged to the priesthood (see 1 Samuel 13:1-15), and then he began to make rash oaths (see 1 Samuel 14:24-30). And the leader who once hid in the baggage now "set up a monument for himself" (1 Samuel 15:12). There are few biblical characters who plummeted as dramatically and tragically as did Saul.

So it became clear that someone must replace Saul. Where does one find a new king? In the palace, obviously, either in the royal family or among the royal confidantes, or perhaps among the military elite. But God chose a different booking agency. He sent Samuel to a farming family near Bethlehem, to anoint their youngest son, who had to be brought in from tending sheep. The plot now centers on David—shepherd boy, slayer of the giant Goliath, sweet singer of Israel, and a man after God's own heart (see 1 Samuel 16–17).

It is with David, it seems to me, that Israel's flag is born. I say that not simply because the symbol of the modern nation of Israel is the Star of David, but because the nation comes into its own with David's ascent to the throne. During the reign of Saul, Israel is still a struggling power, with no standing in the company of surrounding nations. But during David's reign, they gain their place.

David has by far more chapters in the Old Testament than any other single personality. Legends grow naturally around such an individual. It isn't necessarily a case of poor-boy-makes-good, because Jesse, David's father, was apparently a rather successful farmer. But anyone who goes from herding sheep to sitting on the throne is storybook material; and when such a person, late in his career, errs in such a way as to bring suffering to his nation and then remembers his roots so instinctively that he prays, "I alone have sinned, and I alone have done wickedly; but *these sheep*, what have they done?" (2 Samuel 24:17, emphasis added)—well, such a man deserves whatever attention we pay him.

David was a musician, with such gifts that when he played his lyre for King Saul, "Saul would be relieved and feel better, and the evil spirit would depart from him" (1 Samuel 16:23). But David was also a natural athlete, so gifted with his sling that he would dare challenge the Philistine giant, Goliath, and so confident of his abilities that he could convince others to trust the nation's welfare in his hands. But he was more than a strong, simple country boy. When

David heard how the king would reward the person who would defeat the giant, he asked to hear the details repeated: "What shall be done for the man who kills this Philistine?" (1 Samuel 17:26).

David had a gift for friendship. His bonds with King Saul's son, Jonathan, are the stuff of legends in their own right. And during his time of banishment, when he was forced to live by his wits and skills, he gathered to himself some four hundred men, "everyone who was in distress, and everyone who was in debt, and everyone who was discontented" (1 Samuel 22:2). Anyone who can be captain to such a motley, instinctively troublesome group is remarkable, indeed. And with all of this, David was also a poet, and we have every reason to think that women adored him; at any rate, there's no doubt that he was drawn to them.

But I remind myself often of a saying: show me your strength, and I'll show you your weakness. David's gift for people and his natural beauty got him in trouble. He proved at times to be a poor father, because he didn't know how to combine love and discipline. Nor did he know how to discipline himself. The passions that made him lovable also made him susceptible to error. And when he erred, he did so with a flourish.

Nevertheless, David reigned forty years—the first seven over the southern area of his homeland, Judah, and the last thirty-three over the entire nation of Israel. And when he turned the throne over to his son Solomon, Israel was a power to be reckoned with. She was not the largest nation in the Middle East, but her place was secure. In the generations that followed, Israel's historians would use David's reign as the measure of excellence for all his successors; and the prophets would envision the Messiah as someone not only in David's line, but in his love for God.

And when at last Jesus of Nazareth appeared, those who saw him best identified him as "the son of David." But now I'm getting ahead of the story.

5
The People of the Book
Solomon Through Nehemiah/Esther

Kings and Chronicles

As David drew near the end of his reign, there was no question as to his successor. Of course others had an eye on the throne, but David was set on Solomon, the son he had late in life with Bathsheba—the woman with whom he had so dramatically sinned (see 2 Samuel 11–12:24). David remained commander in chief until essentially his last breath, urging Solomon to be courageous, and to keep the statutes, commandments, ordinances, and testimonies "as it is written in the law of Moses" (1 Kings 2:2-3). David also gave Solomon a few items of unfinished business. Above all, David wanted his dream of a temple for the worship of the Lord God to be completed by his son Solomon. As Moses could only stand on Mount Nebo and see the Promised Land from a distance, David could only lay out plans for the temple and trust that Solomon would bring this dream to pass.

No monarch, governor, mayor, or chief executive officer ever made a more auspicious beginning than did Solomon. When, in a dream, God asked Solomon what should be given him, Solomon recalled the nobility of his father, David, and God's faithfulness to him, and acknowledged that by comparison, "I am only a little child"; and with that he pleaded, "Give your servant therefore an understanding mind to govern your people, able to discern between good and evil; for who can govern this your great people?" (1 Kings 3:5-9).

Solomon's prayer was answered. Not only did he gain wisdom to

41

govern his nation, he became known throughout neighboring nations for this wisdom, so that other rulers sought him out, including even the Queen of Sheba, who, having observed his wisdom and the wonders of his reign, could only say, "Not even half had been told me" (1 Kings 10:7). So it is that even into this twenty-first century we speak of the wisdom of Solomon.

But wisdom has irregular borders. It tends to have peculiar blind spots, and sometimes it turns in upon itself. Solomon decided, quite cleverly, that the best way to ensure peace with neighboring nations would be to marry the daughters of their rulers—beginning with the daughter of the pharaoh of Egypt. Obviously, however, Solomon recognized a spiritual issue in what he was doing. He built a separate house for Pharaoh's daughter, because, he said, "My wife shall not live in the house of King David of Israel, for the places to which the ark of the LORD has come are holy" (2 Chronicles 8:11).

But inner compromises of this sort distill the soul. The biblical historian says, "King Solomon loved many foreign women along with the daughter of Pharaoh.... [W]hen Solomon was old, his wives turned away his heart after other gods; and his heart was not true to the LORD his God, as was the heart of his father David" (1 Kings 11:1, 4). Eventually Solomon built altars to panoplies of pagan gods to accommodate his wives, until at last he himself was bowing at the altars of Astarte, Chemosh, and Milcom, the gods of surrounding nations. So the once wisest of men tries in his last years to hold with one hand to the God who chose and empowered him while reaching with the other to mute blocks of wood and stone.

Religion is never an entirely private matter. What one believes in the depths of the soul eventually demonstrates itself in human relationships, business, and government—or to be more correct, in all of life. In the latter years of Solomon's reign, he began making decisions altogether contrary to his early prayer for wisdom in governing God's "great people," so that areas of unrest developed. But Solomon rode on the momentum of his earlier years; the collapse didn't come until his son, Rehoboam, took the throne.

Before I go further, let me explain that as I tell the story of Israel's kings I am drawing upon several biblical books: First and Second Samuel, First and Second Kings, and First and Second Chronicles.

Basically, the books tell the same story but often with emphases of their own. And it is instructive that certain of these books that we would call historical (Joshua, Judges, First and Second Samuel, and First and Second Kings) are classified in the Hebrew Bible as the former prophets, expressing, it seems, the idea that they are looking at history not simply as happenstance events, but as events in which God is strategically involved, and thus events that have about them a prophetic, teaching significance.

Rehoboam has barely come to the throne when Jeroboam, an especially able leader, brings a delegation to appeal the cause of the ten northern tribes. Solomon, Jeroboam explains, had made their lives hard. Would Rehoboam negotiate a better arrangement? Rehoboam asks for three days to consider the request. During those days he consults with a group of older men and with a group from his own generation. Rehoboam goes with the counsel of the younger group, promising that his rule will be far more severe than that of his father. The delegation answers in what sounds so much like a marching song that many Bibles now present it in poetic lines:

> What share do we have in David?
>> We have no inheritance in the son of Jesse.
> To your tents, O Israel!
>> Look now to your own house, O David.
> (1 Kings 12:16)

See how "David" is the symbol of the throne. Some forty years have passed since David's death, and the present occupant of the throne is David's grandson, but it is the house of David, "the son of Jesse."

From this time forward the twelve tribes are two nations. The ten northern tribes are known as Israel, and the southern tribes—Judah and Benjamin—take the name of Judah. A majority of the tribe of Levi is also in the southern confederation, since the Temple is in the city of Jerusalem, in the kingdom of Judah. If you've been doing some adding, it may have occurred to you that we have accumulated thirteen tribes rather than twelve. Here's the explanation. When the Levites were chosen to be the priestly tribe, they lost their land status, as I noted in an earlier chapter. But Joseph had become two tribes through his two sons, Ephraim and Manasseh. When Jacob (also known by the name Israel) was near death, Joseph brought his two sons, Ephraim and Manasseh, to his father for a blessing. Jacob announced that the two sons "who were born to you in the land of Egypt before I came to you in Egypt, are now mine; Ephraim and Manasseh shall be mine, just as Reuben and Simeon are" (Genesis 48:5). In this way, Jacob explained, he was able to give to Joseph "one portion more than to your brothers" (Genesis 48:22). You will note in future listings of the tribes that the name of Joseph is rarely mentioned; rather, Ephraim and Manasseh.

Much of the history that follows is rather bleak—especially for the ten northern tribes. Judah has its good periods, with kings like Asa, Jehoshaphat, Joash, Uzziah, Hezekiah, and Josiah—persons the biblical writer says walked in the way of their father, David. In contrast, when Judah had a wicked king (and they had their share of such), the writer says they were like the kings of Israel. This is because Israel did not have one good king.

By good, I should make clear, the biblical writers are speaking of the ruler's walk with God. Their evaluation has nothing to do with statecraft, political acumen, military exploits, or economic progress. The biblical writer judges rulers entirely on issues of ethics, morals, and spirituality.

And it isn't as though the ten northern tribes didn't have a prophetic witness. They were blessed by the ministry of Elijah, who, although he has left us no written message, is in some respects the most memorable of the Hebrew prophets; and Elijah was succeeded by an equally dramatic and forceful personality, Elisha. Both of these men prophesied almost exclusively in the northern kingdom, and yet the ten tribes never really turned to God. There's something of a message here about the importance of responsible, ethical, godly, political leadership.

But let me talk for a moment about Elijah and Elisha—especially the former. We get a sense of Elijah's significance in the continuing plot when we see how he reappears in the New Testament story. When the angel Gabriel came to Zechariah to announce that Zechariah and Elizabeth would have a son (John the Baptist) who would "make ready a people prepared for the Lord," he said that this son would come with "the spirit and power of Elijah" (Luke 1:17). And when John the Baptist's ministry began to draw crowds and speculation, the people first asked if he might be the Messiah; and when John denied that role, they asked, "What then? Are you Elijah?" (John 1:20-21). Much later, when Jesus was with Peter, James, and John one day, at what we refer to as the Mount of Transfiguration, the two characters who appeared with Jesus were Moses and Elijah—Moses as symbol of the Law, and Elijah as a representative of the prophets (see Matthew 17:1-13; Mark 9:2-13; Luke 9:28-36).

In a sense, Elijah's continuing prominence today seems unlikely. As I said a few moments ago, Elijah left no written documents, so he has no place with prophets such as Isaiah, Jeremiah, Amos, and Hosea. Furthermore, Elijah's ministry during his lifetime could be seen as a failure. He was pitted so often against King Ahab and Queen Jezebel; and although he won some notable victories, Israel never really returned to God in any substantial, continuing way during Elijah's years of ministry and those of his successor, Elisha.

But success—particularly in those issues that matter most—must be measured in a variety of ways. When times are very, very bad, a godly witness succeeds when he keeps the times from being still worse. Sometimes the witness is a voice crying in the wilderness, and a tough-minded critic might ask who, if anyone, is listening out there in the wilderness. And ultimately, of course, the test is simply this: faithfulness. With the odds fearfully against him, Elijah remained faithful. He despaired, mind you, but he remained faithful. In this, Elijah has become the patron saint for those who live in history's more perilous times, and indeed, for any of us when walking a tedious or apparently hopeless road.

As I indicated earlier, the story of the ten northern tribes, Israel, is pretty dismal. In 722 B.C., Assyria, the dominant military power of that era, found Israel easy prey. Assyria not only defeated Israel, they took captive the best of the people, resettling them "in Halah, on the Habor, the River of Gozan, and in the cities of the Medes" (2 Kings 17:5). The biblical historian tells us the story behind the events: "This occurred because the people of Israel had sinned against the LORD their God, who had brought them up out of the land of Egypt from under the hand of Pharaoh king of Egypt" (2 Kings 17:7). A secular voice would have seen the sequence of events as a natural progression of political, military, and economic factors. The biblical historian saw them as spiritual and ethical. In a sense, both interpretations are true. Our moral and ethical conduct affects our politics, our economics, and our relationships both personal and institutional. And yes, the judgment of God is involved: God has given us a moral universe, and if we insist on following immoral patterns, we are at odds with the very structure of our universe. So of course we will suffer.

The pattern of military conquest in those times was to take from any given land the best and ablest people, and to leave behind enough to keep the land from being taken over by wildlife and wild vegetation; then, to bring into the land settlers from other places in the conquering empire. In this instance, Assyria brought into the northern area—Samaria—people from several parts of the empire, and they brought their gods with them. But eventually, as a kind of security measure, the king of Assyria sent back some spiritual leaders from Israel. As the writer of Second Kings summarizes it, "So they worshiped the LORD but also served their own gods, after the manner of the nations from among whom they had been carried away" (2 Kings 17:33). These are the people who will be identified as Samaritans when our story is picked up in the New Testament. This little bit of background will help us understand the longstanding differences between the people of Samaria—once the people of the northern tribes—and the people of Judah.

The people of Judah managed to hold their own in the company of nations for over a century after the northern kingdom, Israel, was taken captive. In that period, Judah had two of her best kings: Hezekiah, whose leadership was much fortified by the prophet Isaiah; and Josiah, who led a spiritual reformation that sprang from a recovery of "the book of the law" (2 Kings 22:8)—which was probably, scholars feel, the book of Deuteronomy. Whatever the biblical book may have been, Josiah found in it an instrument of true repentance for himself and for the people, out of which came a time of remarkable spiritual renewal.

But spiritual vitality has to be born again in every generation, and those who followed Josiah to the throne did not follow him to the place of holy submission. It was only a matter of time until Judah, the southern kingdom, was so corrupt that judgment came upon them "at the command of the LORD, to remove them out of his sight, for the sins of Manasseh, for all that he had committed, and also for the innocent blood that he had shed" (2 Kings 24:3-4). With the passage of time, Babylon had become the dominant military power. After defeating the Assyrians, King Nebuchadnezzar led his Babylonian armies into Jerusalem. There "he carried off all the treasures of the house of the LORD" (spiritually speaking, the ultimate shame), then carried away "all the officials, all the warriors, ten thousand captives, all the artisans and the smiths; no one remained, except the poorest people of the land" (2 Kings 24:13-14). We'll get an idea of the quality of the people taken captive when we read of Daniel, Shadrach, Meshach, and Abednego in the book of Daniel, and of Hadassah (also known as Esther) in the book of Esther.

The prophet Jeremiah had never enjoyed much popularity in Judah: his messages were too dire. Needless to say, when he had predicted that Babylon would invade Judah because of the nation's sins—and thus, that this invasion was of God—no one heeded his warning. Nor did they buy into his promise that someday the land would again be theirs; not even when Jeremiah himself bought a piece of land, assuring the people, "Houses and fields and vineyards shall again be bought in this land" (Jeremiah 32:15). Jeremiah knew how to hope. It would be nearly two generations before his faith became a reality, but he was certain of the ultimate purposes of God.

Daniel and Esther

We include Daniel among the prophetic books of Isaiah, Jeremiah, and Ezekiel. Several of Daniel's chapters report on the faithfulness of God as experienced by a little group of Hebrew boys—I suspect we would call them teenagers. They resolved to be true to their faith in God even though they were in a land where exhibiting such faith invited imprisonment, and even execution. Some scholars feel that these stories were told to Hebrew children to give them the courage to live through periods when their country was occupied by enemy nations. In truth, the people of Judah were remarkably sustained through the period of their captivity—first by the Babylonians, then by the Medes and Persians who conquered the Babylonians.

The book of Esther is set in this latter period—specifically, during the reign of Ahasuerus (Xerxes) (486–465 B.C.). Its basic plot is a familiar one in Israel's history: some enemy of the Jewish people seeks to destroy them, but through divine intervention is himself destroyed. In this instance the intervention comes through the beauty of a Jewish girl, Hadassah (Esther), and her tough-minded, perhaps even obstreperous, older cousin, Mordecai. This book is unique in that the name of God is never mentioned, but events unfold as if choreographed by an unseen, all-knowing power. And so, the purposes of God are fulfilled, and the people of God are preserved. It is in this story that the Jewish people have the basis for their Feast of Purim.

Ezra and Nehemiah

The ten northern tribes of Israel are lost to history sometime in the generations following their conquest by the Assyrians. It doesn't take long for a relatively small people to be swallowed up by a conquering nation, especially a nation as expert in its procedures as the eighth-century-B.C. Assyrians. Thus these tribes are now popularly referred to as the ten lost tribes. Of course such a name has evoked all kinds of speculation.

The marvel, of course, is that the same thing didn't happen to the southern body, Judah. Instead, they are with us to this very day, and this in spite of repeated efforts, large and small, to destroy them as a people. They now bear the name that has come from Judah: Jews. Not only do they continue to exist, they have been and continue to be an astonishing influence on history.

How is it that Judah survived when the ten northern tribes did not? No doubt the Babylonian and Persian governments provided a better setting for survival. Not only that, Judah was much more nourished spiritually. As I indicated earlier, the physical center of faith-celebration, the Temple in Jerusalem, was located within Judah; and while it is true that the people and its rulers often wandered spiritually, there was a place to return. In contrast, Israel's rulers—beginning with Jeroboam—had developed a religious structure of their own. (You will see this issue surface generations later when a first-century resident in Samaria asks Jesus, "Our ancestors worshiped on this mountain, but you say that the place where people must worship is in Jerusalem" [John 4:20].) Also, Judah had the prophet Ezekiel with them in captivity to bolster the spirit of the people with the assurance that their nation would live again.

But especially, Judah had the literature of faith, much of the collection that we now call the Hebrew Scriptures, the Old Testament. And they had two great teachers and leaders in Ezra and Nehemiah. These two men were the primary force as the people of Judah rebuilt their country—their capital city, Jerusalem, with its walls and its place of worship. They led the people with a kind of ferocious intensity. From where we sit, some twenty-five centuries removed, some of their ethnic purging seems brutal; but from where they sat, such ethnic purity was essential to their survival as a people (Ezra 10:16-44).

Nehemiah tells us that the Levites "read from the book, from the law of God, with interpretation. They gave the sense, so that the people understood the reading" (Nehemiah 8:8). And when the people, distressed by what they heard, began to weep, Ezra commanded that the people should be told that "the joy of the LORD is your strength" (Nehemiah 8:10). The Jews were now becoming the people of the Book. Everyone who appreciates the grand literature of the Bible is intellectually indebted to this tiny body of Middle Eastern people. And those of us who have taken Jesus Christ as Lord and who pray for the kingdom of God are both their spiritual debtors and their spiritual heirs. As such, we are privileged to pick up their place in the grand biblical plot.

6
Poets and Philosophers
Job Through Song of Solomon

As you read your Bible, you soon discover that the Old Testament is set up like a small library—which, as a matter of fact, it is. The section we've already covered, Genesis through Esther, is made up of law and history. Although the first five books of the Bible are known to Jewish people as the Torah and to other readers as the Pentateuch (or the books of the Law), they are in a very real sense history, though obviously of a special kind: the story of God's dealing with our human race from the time of Creation through the developing of Israel as a nation, until their restoration as a people in their homeland following the Babylonian and Persian captivities.

Now we come to a place in the holy library that is usually referred to as the Wisdom literature. Most of it is written in the form of poetry. But if you are interested (as I hope you are) in the plot line—God's relationship to our human race—you may feel that poetry and philosophy have little to do with the unfolding of the plot.

Actually, if a plot is to get anywhere, there will have to be some reflecting on life's meaning, significance, and purpose. Sometimes that reflecting comes to us in the form of philosophy—especially political philosophy. One thinks, for example, of Thomas Paine's pamphlet *Common Sense,* or Rousseau's the *Social Contract.* And as for poetry, consider how Julia Ward Howe's "Battle Hymn of the Republic" galvanized a people, or how the American dream was captured in Emma Lazarus's words, "Give me your tired, your poor, / Your huddled masses yearning to breathe free" ("The New Colossus"; 1883). Life's plot is carried in the words of preachers, teachers, and prophets, and in the songs and figures of speech of the poets; and the Eternal Plot is carried, sublimely, in the wisdom of the Scriptures.

But let me interrupt myself to say a few words about biblical poetry. It was Robert Lowth, an eighteenth-century professor of poetry at Oxford University, who first explained the nature of Hebrew poetry. Biblical poetry is structured not around rhyming words or even the rhythm of the lines, but in what Lowth called *parallelism*; that is, lines that make their point in combinations, where the second line (and sometimes a third) complements and fulfills what is declared in the first line. Lowth classified these parallelisms into three types, *synonymous, antithetic,* and *synthetic.*

In the *synonymous* form, the second line makes the same point as the first line, but in different language or figure of speech. For example: "For I know my transgressions, / and my sin is ever before me" (Psalm 51:3). *Antithetical* lines make the same point, but through contrast: "Those who are kind reward themselves, / but the cruel do themselves harm" (Proverbs 11:17). In *synthetic* lines, the second line completes the first or supplements it in some instructive way: "The LORD is my shepherd, / I shall not want" (Psalm 23:1).

This literary form not only gave beauty to the insights and truths the writers were communicating, it also made the material easy to remember. That has virtue in any generation, but especially in a world where writing materials were few. It's easy to imagine ancient Israelites quoting hundreds of lines of the Wisdom literature—material that made the reality of God and the significance of life paramount in their minds.

Job

We know so little about this book except that it is undoubtedly one of the most beautiful pieces of literature ever written. The beginning and the end are in straightforward prose; the remainder is in exquisite poetry. There's a kind of majestic directness, however, even in the prose.

Job was a man in Uz who was "blameless and upright, one who feared God and turned away from evil" (Job 1:1). He was "the greatest of all the people of the east" (1:3), and a person of extraordinary integrity with a devout love for God. Ironically, it was this love for God that got him in trouble. Satan (which means simply "adversary") bargains with God to put Job's character to the test. In an astonishing series of disasters (a kind of cosmic tsunami), Job loses virtually everything: his daughters and sons, his extensive wealth, his health, and his community standing.

In the midst of his loss, Job's friends came to counsel him. Their theology was simple: God will bless the person who does what is right, so if someone is suffering, it's evident that he or she is in the wrong. This is a very common point of view and people in a time of trouble will say, defensively, "What have I done to deserve this?" Or in a sense of guilt, "God is punishing me."

Job refused to be intimidated by his accusers, certain of his innocence before God. Most of the book is occupied with the accusations of Job's "friends" and with his defenses, until at last God takes Job on a whirlwind trip of creation. In truth, God gives Job no answer to the question that is implicit in his suffering, except to make clear that God is God, and God is in control. Job is satisfied with this. "I had heard of you by the hearing of the ear, / but now my eye sees you; / therefore I despise myself, / and repent in dust and ashes" (Job 42:5-6). As the story ends, Job is in every way restored, indeed, he has more at the end than at the beginning: "And Job died, old and full of days" (Job 42:17).

From the earliest days of the church, Christians have read the Old Testament through their own eyes of faith. For such believers, the book of Job offers not only a testimony of God's presence in the midst of life's imponderables, but specific passages in which Christians have found particular significance. In the midst of Job's distress, he cries, "Would that there were an umpire between us, / who might lay his hand on us both" (Job 9:33, footnote with alternate reading). A Christian may see in Job's cry the universal need for One who, like Jesus Christ, can "lay his hand" on both God and humanity.

Job 19:25-27, which is often sung at Easter services, has been interpreted as an Old Testament testimony to the resurrection of the body since at least the writings of Chrysostom (born ca. A.D. 344) and Ephrem the Syrian (born ca. A.D. 306). Thus the plot unfolds, from Old Testament to New, in portraying our profound human need for a Savior who can deal with our human dilemma, and the answer the Christian Scriptures offer in the coming of Jesus Christ.

53

The Psalms

One can judge the value of a book by many measures—its literary beauty, its influence on history, or its place in humanity's intellectual development, for instance. The book of Psalms could be considered under several of those headings, but I choose to identify it as one of the most beloved books in the world. I doubt that any book has been more successful in finding readers in every imaginable culture and in more tongues. Whether the reader is rich or poor, literate or marginal, sophisticated or naïve—indeed, religious or irreligious—he or she is likely to read the Psalms with pleasure and at least some measure of devotion.

This is the longest book in the Bible, with its 150 chapters, plus it contains both the shortest chapter in the Bible (Psalm 117) and the longest (Psalm 119). It is popularly referred to as the psalms of David—King David of Israel, that is—but actually only 73 of the psalms are attributed to him. Over forty are left to that continually popular writer *Anonymous*. And scholars remind us, of course, that the names attached to the psalms are there by way of tradition, and that they may even mean something other than "written by." On the other hand, most readers are happy with the traditional listing of the authors and, even more than that, find they are enriched by the material no matter the author. Perhaps the most significant fact about the psalms is that so many of us feel, as we read, that a particular psalm speaks so intimately to our condition it is as if we, ourselves, had written it.

Some psalms are poignant in their longing for God ("As a deer longs for flowing streams, / so my soul longs for you, O God" [42:1]). Some come from a truly beleaguered soul ("O LORD, how many are my foes! / Many are rising against me" [3:1]). It's interesting to note that the psalm most loved has something of the beleaguered theme ("You prepare a table before me / in the presence of my enemies" [23:5]). The person who recognizes the enormity of his or her sins can find no better words than Psalm 51: "Wash me thoroughly from my iniquity, / and cleanse me from my sin" (51:2). And who, on a day of magnificent natural beauty, but has found just the right words in Psalm 8, "When I look at your heavens, the work of your fingers, / the moon and the stars that you have established; / what are human beings that you are mindful of them, / mortals that you care for them?" (8:3-4).

Dietrich Bonhoeffer, the German theologian who is perhaps more widely known for his fearless opposition to Adolf Hitler, wrote from his prison cell on May 15, 1943, "I am reading the Psalms daily, as I have done for years. I know them and love them more than any other book in the Bible." Bonhoeffer was part of a grand tradition in finding special strength from the psalms during a time when his life was threatened. Numerous Christians have prepared to die, whether naturally or in martyrdom, by reading or quoting the psalms. Psalm 34, in particular, was often chanted by martyrs in the days of Roman persecution. And of course, we do well to remember that two of what we refer to as "the seven last words" of our Lord were quotations from the Book of Psalms: "My God, my God, why have you forsaken me?" (Matthew 27:46; Psalm 22:1); and, "Into your hand I commit my spirit" (Luke 23:46; Psalm 31:5).

The Psalms are the prayer book of the Jewish people, but as scholars and casual observers have noted, we Christians have "baptized the Psalter into Christ." The writers of the New Testament quoted freely from the Psalms, and the generations that have followed have found that this remarkable book not only captures their faith better than almost any other, it also encapsulates their despairs, their longings, their hopelessness, and their hope.

Proverbs

When our generation thinks of wisdom, it is inclined to measure it in academic degrees. Not so with the people who gave us the Old Testament; they saw wisdom as the ability to live life effectively and to do work with excellence. Thus Proverbs tells us that "four things on earth are small, / yet they are exceedingly wise," and gives us not a list of academic leaders, but the ant, the badger, the locust, and the lizard, because these tiny creatures succeed in surviving in their modest world (Proverbs 30:24-28). They are successful in living the life that is given to them.

I tell you this because I know of no better way to prepare us for the counsel that is offered in this remarkable book. There is nothing high-flown or obscure about it; it is as down-to-earth and as accessible as the kind of counsel your grandparents used to give you. We readers are told at the outset that we are about to read "the proverbs of Solomon son of David, king of Israel" (Proverbs 1:1). Before we're done we also have the words of "Agur son of Jakeh" (Proverbs 30) and of the mother of Lemuel (Proverbs 31). It's interesting that the book begins with a father's counsel to his son and concludes with a mother's counsel.

I think it's significant that the Hebrew word for *proverbs* is *chokhmah,* which means quite literally "strong, firm." That is, this book is the kind of foundation on which one can build a life. And I should remind us, too, that the Hebrew has no word for *brain.*[1] They saw the *heart* as the center of the intellect. Of course this means thinking ought to be more than a purely cerebral activity. Perhaps I could say our best thinking is not *coldly* logical, but *warmly* logical. And it implies follow-through. It is practical rather than theoretical, lived-out rather than talked-around.

Very early, in what might be seen as a preamble to the book, the writer tells us quite precisely the essence of what this book is about: "The fear of the LORD is the beginning of knowledge; / fools despise wisdom and instruction" (Proverbs 1:7). As the writer sees it, wisdom isn't hard to find; she "cries out in the street; / in the squares she raises her voice" (Proverbs 1:20). I venture it's more difficult today to hear wisdom's voice—not because she is any less insistent, but because we are distracted and overwhelmed by so many competing voices. And of course we face another problem, too, one that has been faced by every generation: wisdom comes to us with all sorts of demands. If we are to find true wisdom, it will be as we "understand the fear of the LORD / and find the knowledge of God" (Proverbs 2:5).

Wisdom has a sense of humor. "A cheerful heart is a good medicine, / but a downcast spirit dries up the bones" (Proverbs 17:22); no doubt about that. And here's good counsel: "Even fools who keep silent are considered wise" (Proverbs 17:28); I recall numbers of times when I wish I had remembered such counsel. And how about this: "Whoever blesses a neighbor with a loud voice, / rising early in the morning, / will be counted as cursing" (Proverbs 27:14).

This wise man is nothing if not practical! But that's the nature of this book: not abstruse philosophical discussions, but counsel on making good of your life as you find it—the way ants, badgers, locusts, and lizards do.

Ecclesiastes

In some respects no book of wisdom is more appropriate to our times here in the western world than the book of Ecclesiastes. This book gives us the philosophical pilgrimage of a person who had everything and could only say, "Vanity of vanities! All is vanity" (Ecclesiastes 1:2).

He gives us a play-by-play report, but with the warning, "All things are wearisome; / more than one can express; / the eye is not satisfied with seeing, / or the ear filled with hearing" (Ecclesiastes 1:8). He tries wisdom, but finds that "in much wisdom is much vexation" (1:18). So he turns to pleasure, with homes, vineyards, and pools, and also "delights of the flesh," with "many concubines." But it is all "a chasing after wind" (2:1-11). He is grieved as he realizes that "there is no enduring remembrance of the wise or of fools, seeing that in the days to come all will have been long forgotten" (2:16).

He struggles to find a higher philosophical ground, reminding us that there is "a time to be born, and a time to die; / a time to plant, and a time to pluck up what is planted" (3:2). And he's right when he tells us that "two are better than one . . . for if they fall, one will lift up the other" (4:9-10). We agree with him when he says, "A good name is better than precious ointment," but he seems pretty heavy when he continues, "and the day of death, than the day of birth" (7:1).

In simplest terms, what seems to bother this wise man the most is his conclusion that "the same fate comes to all, to the righteous and the wicked, to the good and the evil" (9:2). He has no perception of a life beyond this one, so he sees no possibility of a final ordering of accounts. He believes there ought to be justice in this universe, and he can't find it.

As the book ends, he makes an appeal to his readers: "Remember your creator in the days of your youth, before the days of trouble come, and the years draw near when you will say, 'I have no pleasure in them'" (12:1). At last he says, "The end of the matter; all has been heard. Fear God, and keep his commandments; for that is the whole duty of everyone. For God will bring every deed into judgment, including every secret thing, whether good or evil" (12:13-14). Some scholars feel that this end was tacked on later. They find it so contrary to the rest of the book that they're sure the original author couldn't have said it. Personally, I find the book's conclusion altogether logical. After this poor yuppie has tried everything, after he has traveled the earth and his 513 television channels, he turns desperately to where he should have started: fear God and keep his commandments. I don't think everyone who has so much and feels so frustrated ends up where this man did, but I suspect the reason he finished his journey with a modicum of faith-sense is because even at the start, when he began telling us of his "unhappy business," he included God in the equation (1:13). And though he took a long, rather ugly journey to find a conclusion, he realized in the end that there is God, and we had better trust that God will "bring every deed into judgment."

And perhaps there's a sense in which the pervasive cry of this book ("Everything is vanity"), based on the thinking that death, "the same fate," comes to all, is a kind of prophecy in petition: a cry for the reality of eternal life that is fully declared in the New Testament.

Song of Solomon

When I tell you that the Song of Solomon is a love song, you may well wonder how it fits into a section of Wisdom literature. We sometimes have the feeling, as we look at friends or family or novels or movies—or for that matter, our own lives—that people in love are more likely to be out of their wits than studies in wisdom.

In a sense, the Song of Solomon will do little to disabuse you of such an idea. When a book begins, "Let him kiss me with the kisses of his mouth! / For your love is better than wine" (1:2), you have a feeling you're dealing with emotions, not intellect. And nothing later in the book will change your mind. This book is about two people wonderfully in love, with their feelings recorded by a master poet. You may not always appreciate his figures of speech, when he says that his beloved's hair "is like a flock of goats," and her cheeks "like halves of a pomegranate" (4:1, 3), but remind yourself that we always use figures of speech from the world in which we live, and for someone in a world dominated by agriculture and nature, the poet's language is eloquent indeed.

And sometimes his language leaps all cultural barriers, as when he writes, "Many waters cannot quench love, / neither can floods drown it. / If one offered for love / all the wealth of his house, / it would be utterly scorned" (8:7).

Rabbinical scholars often interpreted this book as a record of God's love for Israel, and Christian scholars as God's love for the church. But neither thought should distract from the very beautiful and quite candid expression of human love. And if such a book seems out of place in the literature of wisdom, perhaps this suggests both that love ought more often to include an element of wisdom, and that our wisdom ought more often to have elements of wonder, beauty, and ecstasy.

---

[1]John Paterson, *The Book That Is Alive* (New York: Charles Scribner's Sons, 1954), page 56: "Hebrew has no word for brain and the heart was the organ of intellection."

7

Truth and Consequences
Isaiah Through Malachi

Many of us approach the prophetic books of the Old Testament with a preconception that can easily frustrate our understanding. We see *prophecy* as a predictive word and therefore look at these books, from Isaiah through Malachi, as messages that have been fulfilled or that are awaiting fulfillment.

This predictive factor is, of course, one element in the prophetic books. But it is not the only element; and it may in fact occupy far fewer pages than the other prophetic expression. Teachers have sometimes said that the prophetic books *foretell* and *forthtell;* that is, sometimes they predict, and sometimes they preach. I'd like to put it this way: the work of the prophets was sometimes to *correct the present* (preaching), and sometimes to *lift up the future* (predicting). But in either case, they always speak with both present and eternal significance.

We customarily divide these books into the major prophets (Isaiah through Daniel) and minor prophets (Hosea through Malachi). This classification has nothing to do with the merits of the several books but simply with their length. There's surely nothing minor, for example, about Hosea and Amos.

We also refer to these books as the written prophets. As we noticed earlier, Elijah, one of the most revered of the Hebrew prophets, has no place in this collection; apparently, all of his work was oral. So, too, with his successor, Elisha. Nor do we have anything from the prophetess Huldah, though she played an extraordinarily significant role in a revival in the days of King Josiah. And although we usually think of the prophets as quite independent personalities who sometimes appeared on the scene without warning and left it without notice, there were schools of the prophets at some points in biblical history, as in the days of Elijah and Elisha, and these schools represented both organization and continuity.

It's easy to think of prophets as a corrective to the more structured ministry of the priests and Levites. Where the temple worship was orderly and ritualistic, the prophets seem spontaneous and untrammeled. It's also easy to see the prophets as outsiders, always at odds with the establishment. There's truth in both of these perceptions, but not the whole truth. Some of the prophets, like Ezekiel, came from the tribe of Levi, and while it's natural to think of a competition between the prophets and the priests, there isn't much evidence to support the idea. As for their being outsiders, some—like Isaiah—were very near the establishment, and even the most independent of the prophets were often called in to confer with the kings. Most of the biblical kings, even at their worst, were spiritual enough to seek out the prophets in times of confusion or trouble. King Zedekiah generally "did what was evil in the sight of the LORD" (2 Chronicles 36:12); nevertheless he sent for the prophet Jeremiah so he could ask, "Is there any word from the LORD?" (Jeremiah 37:17).

This was the prophets' stock in trade—a word from the Lord—and they offered it freely, including occasions when it wasn't welcome. We quote them still today, more than twenty-five centuries after they spoke and wrote. I find that the seventeenth edition of *Bartlett's Familiar Quotations* has 185 citations from the prophets, with particular attention to the prophet Isaiah.

I see the prophets as wonderfully practical persons whose customary aim was to correct or comfort their own generations. Sometimes they corrected by looking at the future in a style that said, "If you continue living as you are now, you're heading for trouble because the judgment of God is going to fall." And when they comforted, it was usually by the same looking to the future, except that now they were saying, "Better days (indeed, superb days!) are coming." A preacher who hopes to be effective can learn from this example. We humans need sometimes to be told that we are wrong and at other times to be embraced. The prophets were effective at both levels, though it's clear that their audiences liked them better when they were promising, "They will not hurt or destroy / on all my holy mountain" (Isaiah 11:9), than when they said, "Woe to him who builds his house by unrighteousness" (Jeremiah 22:13).

Sometimes the prophetic utterances are nothing more than holy common sense: if you continue in this sinful path, you will destroy yourselves. But I'm sure that sometimes the prophets were speaking beyond their human knowledge, and they themselves had no idea of the magnitude of their words. When we get into the New Testament, we will discover that the Christian writers, from Matthew to Revelation, saw it as their responsibility to explain what the prophets had in mind. So it is that the prophets throw out hints as to where the plot is going, and the New Testament writers, while telling their story, pause at times to say, "Do you remember what the prophets said? Now you see it happening."

Isaiah

But it's time to get into some of the particular prophets, beginning with the majestic person of Isaiah. Many scholars have concluded that the book of Isaiah was written by two, and perhaps even three, different persons. I won't go into this discussion, because our understanding of the book and the benefit we receive from its message is not really affected by the number of authors.

Rather early in the book, Isaiah tells of a vision he received at the time of the death of King Uzziah, one of Judah's long-reigning monarchs. Surely the vision influenced the writer, but one can only guess how it shaped the book. So, too, we are told at the beginning that the prophet ministered in the days of four kings, Uzziah, Jotham, Ahaz, and Hezekiah. We know how much the prophet influenced King Hezekiah (see Isaiah 36–39), but we don't really know how these kings may have influenced the prophet or his message. In its sixty-six chapters, the book of Isaiah finds a broader base and a grander vision than these kings would themselves provide.

Isaiah is the first of the prophets to be quoted in the New Testament. After Matthew has reported the angel's visit to Joseph, he goes on to say, "All this took place to fulfill what had been spoken by the Lord through the prophet," at which point Matthew quotes

Isaiah 7:14 (Matthew 1:22-23). But in the story of the birth of our Lord, the passage from Isaiah that is probably quoted most often is Isaiah 9:2-7. Among Christmas cards with a religious motif, the line used most often is from Luke ("Glory to God in the highest heaven, / and on earth peace among those whom he favors" [Luke 2:14]), while next would be the words of Isaiah describing a coming ruler as "the Prince of Peace" (Isaiah 9:6), a title that traditionally has been applied to Jesus. It is interesting that this phrase from an Old Testament prophet is woven so intensely into our Christmas celebration. Indeed, I suspect that a majority of our Advent and Christmas programs include excerpts from the prophet Isaiah. Certainly Handel's *Messiah* relies heavily on excerpts from Isaiah.

Isaiah's words are also prominent in our celebration of the other most significant period in the church calendar, Holy Week. In this instance, the quotations come from Isaiah 52 and 53, the section we often refer to as "The Suffering Servant." Some biblical scholars interpret this passage as describing the role of the nation of Israel in the community of humankind. One can't really say what the prophet himself had in mind. But New Testament writers refer to this chapter ten times in their interpretation of the suffering of Jesus. (For a listing, see *The New Interpreter's Study Bible*, page 1012.) Whatever the prophet may have thought in writing this graphically moving passage, the church has felt from the first century that, knowingly or not, Isaiah was describing the redemptive suffering of Jesus Christ.

For people who are only peripherally acquainted with the Bible, however—those who know only a few verses that they may not even be able to locate, or who quote some familiar phrases without knowing they are quoting the Bible—Isaiah may be known best through some of the majestic promises of a better day still to come. "The wolf shall live with the lamb, / the leopard shall lie down with the kid, / the calf and the lion and the fatling together, / and a little child shall lead them" (Isaiah 11:6). Or, "The spirit of the Lord GOD is upon me, / because the LORD has anointed me; / he has sent me to bring good news to the oppressed, / to bind up the brokenhearted, / to proclaim liberty to the captives" (Isaiah 61:1). Isaiah saw so very, very much. Our planet is still waiting for some of Isaiah's vision to become reality. The plot, that is, is still unfolding, and a grand seer more than twenty-five centuries ago was utterly confident that someday it would come.

Jeremiah

If Isaiah was the prince of the prophets, Jeremiah was given a more painful role. We call him "the weeping prophet," because he said of himself, "O that my head were a spring of water, / and my eyes a fountain of tears, / so that I might weep day and night / for the slain of my poor people!" (Jeremiah 9:1). This prophet has left his mark on our vocabulary: *jeremiad is* a mournful complaint.

Jeremiah's call came when he was young; he said, in fact, "I am only a boy" (1:6). But God answered, "Now I have put my words in your mouth. / See, today I appoint you over nations and over kingdoms, / to pluck up and to pull down, / to destroy and to overthrow, / to build and to plant" (1:9-10). Announcing the overthrow of nations is a dramatic assignment, and Jeremiah found that it came at a high price—especially when he had to pronounce judgments on his own beloved nation. Few cries are more heartrending than Jeremiah's "You will be in the right, O LORD, / when I lay charges against you; / but let me put my case to you. / Why does the way of the guilty prosper? / Why do all who are treacherous thrive?" (12:1). At one point Jeremiah accused God of enticing and overpowering him, so that he resolved he would not speak in God's name again; but "then within me there is something like a burning fire / shut up in my bones; / I am weary with holding it in, / and I cannot" (20:9).

Not only did Jeremiah have to declare that the Babylonians would invade Judah, he also insisted that the people should not resist the invading army, since what was happening was a judgment from God. He told them that in their captivity they should "seek the welfare of the city where I [God] have sent you into exile, and pray to the LORD on its behalf, for in its welfare you will find your welfare" (29:7). This was the kind of preaching that brought persecution on Jeremiah and that caused his people to see him as a traitor. And yet Jeremiah was so sure of Judah's ultimate future under God that in the midst of Babylon's siege, he bought a piece of land: "For thus says the

LORD of hosts, the God of Israel: Houses and fields and vineyards shall again be bought in this land" (32:15). Perhaps the height of Jeremiah's spiritual insight comes when he promises that a day is coming when God's covenant with Israel will be a "law within them," written by God "on their hearts; and I will be their God, and they shall be my people" (31:33).

Lamentations

Lamentations is a short book that apparently comes out of the same period of the Babylonian invasion of Judah and the destruction of the Temple. "How lonely sits the city / that once was full of people" (1:1). The sorrow of the writer is profound. It is not only that houses and government buildings and the Temple itself are demolished; worse, most of the people either have fled or have been taken captive, and it appears that God has forsaken the people.

But in the midst of the loss, the writer lifts his head in a declaration of faith like Job's: "The steadfast love of the LORD never ceases, / his mercies never come to an end; / they are new every morning; / great is your faithfulness" (3:22-23).

Ezekiel

Where Jeremiah ministered to the people before and during the Babylonian invasion, Ezekiel was their spiritual leader in captivity. As I mentioned earlier, Ezekiel was himself a priest. I see him therefore as both worship leader and exhorter. He had the unenviable task of helping his people understand their defeat, including the loss of their holy city and its Temple, and their deportation to another country. For a nation that annually celebrated its deliverance from Egypt, the idea of a new exile must have been unthinkable.

It seems to me, therefore, that Ezekiel's key vision is the one recorded in chapter 37, when he finds himself in a valley of dry bones, where God asks if these bones—obviously symbolic of Israel—can live. God's promise to Ezekiel, and through him to his nation, is this: "I am going to open your graves, and bring you up from your graves, O my people; and I will bring you back to the land of Israel. And you shall know that I am the LORD, when I open your graves, and bring you up from your graves, O my people" (Ezekiel 37:12-13). The last nine chapters of the book describe the restored people, with a new Temple and a new land, and with God in their midst.

Daniel

The book of Daniel combines Daniel's prophetic visions with the stories of Daniel and his friends Shadrach, Meshach, and Abednego, after their deportation from Israel to Babylon. The heroic miracle stories of Daniel and his friends were meant to encourage the Jews in their exile, just as they have inspired scores of generations—especially the young—in a variety of difficulties both great and small. Anyone who has not heard the stories of the four young men (probably teenagers, by our measure), who refused the king's diet in order to be true to their God, and the story of the three who went into a fiery furnace for their faith, or the story of the aged Daniel thrown into the lions' den for his convictions, is poor in the literature of holy courage.

Some of Daniel's visions are reflected in the language and visions of the New Testament book of Revelation. In the Hebrew Bible, Daniel is found not among the prophets but in the section known as "The Writings," which includes such books as the Psalms, Ruth, Esther, Ezra, and Nehemiah.

Minor Prophets

Hosea is the first of the twelve books we often refer to as the Minor Prophets, though I note again that there is nothing minor about their messages. In the Hebrew Bible they are bound together, sometimes referred to as "the Book of the Twelve."

In its dramatic way Hosea portrays the love of God as memorably as any book in the Bible. The prophet Hosea receives his message through his own marital experience, and God explains to the wounded prophet that Israel and Judah have rejected God just as Hosea's wife has rejected him. "When Israel was a child," God tells

A HOP, SKIP, AND A JUMP THROUGH THE BIBLE

Hosea, "I loved him, / and out of Egypt I called my son. / The more I called them, / the more they went from me" (Hosea 11:1-2). Few passages in the Bible have more pathos than God's cry to and through Hosea: "How can I give you up, Ephraim? / How can I hand you over, O Israel?" (11:8).

Joel dates his message, not by the usual reference to reigning kings, but by a natural disaster, a locust invasion. He sees the tragedy as a time of judgment, but not without hope: "Yet even now, says the LORD, / return to me with all your heart, / with fasting, with weeping, and with mourning; / rend your hearts and not your clothing. / Return to the LORD, your God, / for he is gracious and merciful, / slow to anger, and abounding in steadfast love, / and relents from punishing" (Joel 2:12-13). The apostle Peter quotes the prophet Joel during his sermon on the Day of Pentecost (see Acts 2:17-21). So, again, the continuing tie between the two Testaments and the continuing realization of an unfolding plot. What Joel envisions hundreds of years earlier, Peter sees unfolding in his own day.

Amos, as a person, is one of the most fascinating of the prophets. By trade a herdsman and a dresser of sycamore trees and not a prophet nor a prophet's son, he had nevertheless been called by God to prophesy. Worse, a resident of Judah, he had been called to prophesy in Israel, the northern kingdom. Amos's appeal for true religion is one of the most impassioned to be found anywhere, as he reports God's message:

> I hate, I despise your festivals,
>   and I take no delight in your solemn assemblies.
> Even though you offer me your burnt offerings and grain
>   offerings,
>   I will not accept them;
> and the offerings of well-being of your fatted animals
>   I will not look upon.
> Take away from me the noise of your songs;
>   I will not listen to the melody of your harps.
> But let justice roll down like waters,
>   and righteousness like an ever-flowing stream. (Amos 5:21-24)

Obadiah, the shortest of the Old Testament books, deals with a matter that may seem distant and minor to us. The Edomites, the descendants of Esau, Jacob's brother, were cousins, so to speak, to Israel. When some of the Jews fled Jerusalem during the Babylonian invasion, Edom turned them over to the Babylonians. "For the slaughter and violence done to your brother Jacob, / shame shall cover you, / and you shall be cut off forever" (Obadiah 10).

For the casual student of the Bible, **Jonah** may be the best known of the minor prophets—not for his message but for his parabolic experience. I like to say that Jonah was the prophet who discovered the world. He learned to his dismay that God loves even wicked people and is anxious for them to repent. Jonah found this hard to accept and the book concludes without indicating whether he accepted the message. It ends that way because readers should make that decision in their own lives.

Micah was probably a peasant farmer. His message is as powerful a statement for justice as can be found, and he has been quoted by politicians and reformers for generations. He cries out against those who "covet fields, and seize them" and who "oppress householder and house" (Micah 2:2). He is especially grieved that his nation's "priests teach for a price, / its prophets give oracles for money; / yet they lean upon the LORD and say, / 'Surely the LORD is with us!'" (3:11).

Then Micah challenges us with a grand rhetorical question: "He has told you, O mortal, what is good; / and what does the LORD require of you / but to do justice, and to love kindness, / and to walk humbly with your God?" (6:8). In those few words we have a message for every generation, every political body, every ruler, and every individual human being.

The book of **Nahum** is not dated in any way, so scholars date it by its reference to the fall of Nineveh. The prophet rejoices in the judgment that the Assyrians have suffered, because he feels they are being punished for their brutality to others. At the same time, Nahum seems to warn his own people that similar judgment could come to them if they do not pursue righteousness.

The prophet **Habakkuk** faces a double problem. At first he is grieved by the wickedness of his people, Judah, and feels they should be brought to judgment; then he learns that judgment is indeed coming, but through the Chaldeans (Babylon), which makes him ask how God can be silent "when the wicked swallow / those more righteous than they?" (Habakkuk 1:13). The prophet is told that "the righteous live by their faith" (2:4), a phrase that the apostle Paul picks up in his exposition on justification by faith (see Romans 1:17 and Galatians 3:11). This phrase was also key in Martin Luther's Reformation message.

In one sense, the prophecy of **Zephaniah** is confusing. He is writing in the time of King Josiah, one of the most godly of Judah's kings, yet he predicts "a day of distress and anguish, / a day of ruin and devastation, / a day of darkness and gloom" (1:15) because the people "have sinned against the LORD" (1:17). Was Zephaniah looking farther down the road, envisioning wickedness beyond Josiah's time? Or did he sense that the repentance and piety of the people were not deep enough to sustain the spiritual life of the people, and because of this superficiality, fearful judgment would come? Zephaniah appeals to the "humble of the land" (2:3)—surely the best hope for true spiritual renewal—and promises a day "when I restore your fortunes / before your eyes, says the LORD" (3:20).

Haggai and **Zechariah** deal with the same issue, though with different style. The Jews had returned from the Babylonian/Persian captivity and had begun rebuilding their nation, but they had forsaken their work on the Temple for a number of years. Haggai puts the matter directly: "Is it a time for you yourselves to live in your paneled houses, while this house [the Temple] lies in ruins?" (1:4). Zechariah deals with the same issues in a series of often exotic visions, then later with grand oracles. Haggai was successful in that the people responded by pouring new energy and resources into the Temple's restoration.

You will find in the book of Zechariah one of the loveliest prophetic promises to be found anywhere: "Thus says the LORD of hosts: Old men and old women shall again sit in the streets of Jerusalem, each with staff in hand because of their great age. And the streets of the city shall be full of boys and girls playing in its streets" (8:4-5). The caliber of any civilization or any government will always be measured by its treatment of the most defenseless elements in its population, the very young and the very old.

Malachi, the last of the prophets, is undated. His name, too, raises a question, since Malachi means "my messenger" and may therefore only be a kind of title rather than the name of the author. It's clear that the book comes from the Persian period. Events suggest it was from the time of Nehemiah's second arrival in Jerusalem. Its ending seems a perfect transition to the New Testament, since it predicts a return of the prophet Elijah (4:5), the role fulfilled by John the Baptist.

As we embarked on this chapter, I said that the prophets were both foretellers and forthtellers: that they sometimes predicted (without necessarily knowing the reach of their message) and that they sometimes simply exhorted their contemporaries to repent.

But whether predicting or exhorting, the prophets were always looking to the future in their preaching. After all, if we are urged to mend our ways and we do so, we affect the future most beautifully.

The Bible is a book that loves the future, and that encourages all who read it to love the future, because the Bible believes in redemption. It tells us that under God, we humans and the institutions we establish can change, and that God is constantly calling us to wholesome change. The prophets were passionate in this conviction. Even in their darkest struggles, they were supremely optimistic about God's role in the denouement of our human story. We do well to listen to them and then to rise up and follow them in God's call.

8

The Plot Takes
on New Dimensions

Introduction to the New Testament

W HEN WE CHRISTIANS FINISH READING THE OLD TESTAMENT, WE'RE
impatient to get on with the story. As a result, we're quite happy to
skip over the centuries that separate Haggai, Zechariah, and
Malachi from the New Testament writers so that we can get into the
story of the birth, ministry, and teachings of our Lord.

For the Jews, however, this period involved some fierce struggles
for survival; and as far as human judgment could see, the Eternal
Plot was surely in peril. As we noted earlier, the Persians who succeeded Babylon as rulers of the Jews were relatively kind in their
treatment of subjected peoples, perhaps especially the Jews. So, too,
was Alexander the Great. But the Seleucid Empire, one of the states
that came out of Alexander's empire, was another matter. King
Antiochus IV (Epiphanes) was a passionate nationalist; he insisted
that the several nations in his domain become fully Greek in culture
and customs. This could be difficult enough for any ethnic group to
accept, but for the most devout Jews it was unthinkable, although
some of course gave in. But the conflict rose to a new level in 168 or
167 B.C., when Antiochus entered Jerusalem, built an altar to the
Greek god Zeus in the Temple itself, and decreed the death penalty
for circumcising a child, observing the Sabbath, or owning sacred
books. For the devout, it was now a matter of resist, or cease to exist
as a faith-people.

Judas Maccabeus led a small force against a much larger, better
equipped Seleucid army until 165 B.C., when he reentered

Jerusalem, cleansed the Temple, and rededicated it to its ancient commitments. The Jewish feast of Hanukkah was born in the events of this struggle. But after Judas Maccabeus's death in battle five years later, the Jewish people continued to be subject to the powerful military and political structures of much larger nations, so that at the time of the birth of Jesus their country was simply a minor state within the burgeoning Roman Empire.

No matter. Whatever the power of invading nations, the dreams of the Jews lived on. Thus when John the Baptist began preaching early in the New Testament story, people were soon speculating whether he might be the Messiah, the one who would deliver Israel from her oppressors.

Let me interrupt our visit long enough to marvel once again that the writings that we call the Old Testament managed to survive this period. I consider this survival a miracle in its own right. If these books had been stored only in the grand library at Alexandria, Egypt—a collection that sought to include a copy of every known scroll in existence, and that came to have more than 400,000—the books of the Old Testament would be lost today. There is not a trace of the Alexandrian Library, and we can only wonder what happened to it. Meanwhile, there was this relatively small, frequently harassed people, ordered to destroy their sacred literature or be executed for owning it, and still their literature is among us today. Remarkable, to say the least. And it was from faithful study of their literature that many of the devout nurtured their expectation that the Messiah would come, and that they would recognize him when he appeared.

There were many political and religious movements within Israel at the time. Some rose up and died so quickly that little record remains. It seems entirely possible that archaeologists will someday stumble upon some equivalent of the Dead Sea Scrolls, where we learn about the Essenes, and we will learn then of still another first-century sect of Judaism.

But broadly speaking, I'd like to suggest that three major groups existed when our Lord began his ministry. In many ways the most respected were the Pharisees. They were terribly in earnest, and they meant to keep the biblical law. We are right in avoiding the self-righteousness that so sadly marked their conduct, but we would do well to recognize that all of us are susceptible to our own expressions of self-righteousness. The Pharisees felt it was their duty to explain and interpret the law, and in their own way they pleaded the cause of the common people, though one senses that they didn't really understand the simple people of the land, and therefore they were never really comfortable with them.

The Sadducees were the people in power in first-century Judaism. They ruled the Temple, which was a profitable enterprise, and they acquiesced to the Roman government knowing that if they opposed the Romans they would lose their power. A dramatic theological difference between the Pharisees and the Sadducees is that the Pharisees believed in the resurrection of the body, while the Sadducees did not.

And then there were what the rulers called "the people of the earth." They were the common people—fishermen, craftsmen, day laborers (remember Jesus' parable about the workers hired in the marketplace for a day's work?), and farmers. Numerically, they were the largest portion of the population, but they had no political or economic clout, and certainly no intellectual standing. It is of these that the Bible speaks when it refers to the "common people" who heard Jesus "gladly." And primarily it was on such as these that our Lord built the church. Is this where you would begin if you hoped to build a worldwide institution that would still be in existence two thousand years later? Does a body of people such as this strike you as the best potential to continue an eternal story?

And We Began to Have Another Book

The Old Testament was written over a period of a thousand years or more, and it is altogether likely that portions were preserved in oral memory for generations before being put into writing. The New Testament, conversely, was written in something like forty or fifty years. It is a document almost as old as the movement on which it reports. If we could divest ourselves of the kind of holy caution that tends to mark our reading of the Bible, at times our composure would be taken from us by the almost breathless way the New Testament writers tell their story. They are still in the midst of the church's birth pangs. Luke is writing the book of Acts even as the latter chapters unfold, so that sometimes Acts sounds almost like a diary. The letters (epistles) are wrestling with immediate issues that must be dealt with as quickly as a messenger can take the apostolic letter back to the congregation or the individual. And although the Gospels were written a generation after the events, they have about them the same pulsating, almost childlike excitement.

I should also note that the first century was a period of great volatility, in the culture in general, and particularly in the newborn movement that we now call the church. It seems there are periods in history when the marketplace of ideas is rife with excitement. The first century was one of those periods. Thus, on the one hand, the message of Jesus Christ undoubtedly got a readier hearing than it might have known in other times; I think I will call this providential. And perhaps it is just as providential that, on the other hand, because of the fervent clutter of ideas, the church had to deal with potential heresies within its first two generations. Paul's Letter to the Galatians answers the continuing issue of grace versus works in the plan of salvation. The First Letter of John rejects the Gnosticism that was invading the church—a kind of thinking not unlike what we call New Age in our day. As we see the New Testament writers answering some of these erratic teachings, we can be properly warned that truth is always at battle; we need not be surprised or disheartened by this fact.

Let me say a little about how the books of the New Testament came into existence. The first books of the New Testament to be written were the Epistles—that is, those letters that were sent to particular congregations or individuals. The earliest was almost surely Paul's First Letter to the Thessalonians. Scholars date this letter at A.D. 50. This means that it was written about twenty years after the crucifixion and resurrection of our Lord. The church was very young. Scattered through the Roman Empire were literally thousands of persons who had seen Jesus in the flesh and who had heard him preach, and hundreds who had walked on the road outside Jerusalem on the day he was crucified. Indeed, in a later letter the apostle Paul says that many still living were among five hundred who had seen Jesus after his resurrection (1 Corinthians 15:6).

I will say more about the Epistles in a later chapter. At this point I want only to make a few passing comments. These letters are a remarkable testimony to the historicity of the Christian faith and its teachings. As we read them we become members of the first generation of Christians, sitting with them in the homes where they worshiped together or at the riverside or some other simple meeting place; and in some instances, during periods of persecution (which were sporadic and frequent) in places where they met secretly. The letters have a simple authenticity that compels our attention. They aren't the product of an advertising agency or a public relations firm, nor are they carefully crafted defenses of the faith or evangelistic documents that are intended to win new converts. Indeed, an inquirer who was interested in exploring Christianity might easily have concluded that he or she wanted nothing to do with a group facing so many problems. The fact is, these letters never would have been written except that these early congregations—and in some instances (as with the letters to Timothy and Titus) the persons working with them— were facing problems, seeking answers to questions, or needing help to keep going. Only the letter to the Romans was a somewhat organized explanation of the faith; the rest were written to deal with particular problems, concerns, or questions.

Paul and the other apostolic leaders must have written many such letters. We can hardly guess how many, but we have some evidence. For example, in Paul's First Letter to the Corinthians, he refers to an earlier letter (1 Corinthians 5:9) of which we have no record. Then in his second letter, he speaks of what is apparently still another letter (2 Corinthians 2:1–4) that we do not have. And who can imagine how often an early leader wrote to other believers, whether as congregation or as individuals, to answer questions, to encourage discipleship, to reprove (for they took their faith seriously enough to accept tough judgments), or to clarify issues of faith?

As I said earlier, the first of Paul's letters was written in A.D. 50. According to current biblical scholarship, the earliest Gospel, Mark, was probably written in A.D. 70. But within that same decade, Luke's Gospel was written, and its author begins, "Since many have undertaken to set down an orderly account of the events that have been fulfilled among us, just as they were handed on to us by those who from the beginning were eyewitnesses and servants of the word, I too decided, after investigating everything carefully from the very first, to write an orderly account" (Luke 1:1-3).

Two things impress us as we read Luke's words. First, that by that time "*many*" had "undertaken to set down an orderly account." So I repeat the question I asked earlier: how many are *many*? More than four, surely! Again, one can only imagine how many persons might have attempted to record their experiences with Jesus or what they had heard from others of his story. One thinks immediately of those persons who had special contact with him—like the woman who was healed of her issue of blood, or the man whose daughter was raised from the dead, or the woman taken in adultery, or the boy whose small lunch fed thousands. And of course there would be those late-comers who never saw Jesus in the flesh but who heard the story from firsthand witnesses and who possessed enough literary skill to want to compose the story for their own keeping and for sharing with friends.

Also, one is impressed that Luke insists that the persons who communicated the story must be those "who from the beginning were eyewitnesses and servants of the word." The persons recording the story might not be eyewitnesses, but they must get their data only from such individuals; that is, they were not working from hearsay. The story of Jesus the Christ was far too important to their lives and much too crucial in its details to be treated casually, no matter how enthusiastic and sincere the reporters might be. Not many of the first believers were learned persons, but they had encountered One who was the embodiment of Truth, and therefore they must not taint him with falsehood; and because they also knew him as the Word, they treated with sacredness the words they used to tell his story. This is something of the significance I see in Luke's description of the witnesses as being "servants of the word." The story was to use *them,* rather than their using the story.

If those of us who read the New Testament lesson in a Sunday worship service were to grasp the significance and power of the words we're about to read, we would warn our congregations, "Fasten your seat belts! We're about to take quite a ride!"

THE PLOT TAKES ON NEW DIMENSIONS

John Bertram Phillips, an Anglican rector who was serving a London parish during World War II, was trying to sustain his congregation through the nightly air raids by teaching them the Epistles. When they struggled to understand difficult language, Phillips would paraphrase—a practice that eventually led to his translating the entire New Testament, the first "modern English" attempt in the twentieth century. As he worked with the Greek in which the New Testament was originally written, he began to realize the "sheer power of the deceptively simple Greek." He found the material "so alive," he realized that "you must accept the challenge of its intrinsic authority or leave it alone."

And he also realized the power that caused the early church to survive, making them "a triumphant rock in the surrounding pagan world." Phillips was confident that such a triumphant faith could be reborn in us today "in the acceptance of the New Testament itself."[1]

Now and again when people refer to the Bible as the Word of God, someone will counter that Jesus is the Word of God, and that the Bible is a book that tells us about God. I understand the point intended by such a response, but I wouldn't want such a concept, valid as it is, to minimize the importance and the authority of the Bible and its role. Let me suggest that the Bible relates to Jesus in this way: that the Old Testament prepares us for Jesus' coming (thus, the first Christians found all they knew or needed to know about Jesus in the Hebrew Scriptures), while the New Testament tells the story of Jesus, his ministry, and his teachings. That is, the Old and New Testaments serve as the bookends around the eternal fact of Jesus, the Word.

So we're ready now to move on with the plot. Let's put it this way. All through the Old Testament we have seen God at work in the world: particularly through the nation Israel and her history, through prophets like Isaiah, Hosea, and Amos, and through wise men and women who gave us the Psalms, Proverbs, and the book of Job. Through it all, with an extraordinary variety of circumstances and personalities, even violence, war, and general misadventure, God has been at work, pursuing the world with untiring love.

Now it is time in our unfolding story for God to make the most dramatic move of all. The Old Testament has been telling us a story that is momentous in its own right. But now God, very God, is going to move into the story by way of the divine Son, Jesus Christ. This is the breathtaking news we will find awaiting us in the New Testament.

---

[1]Denis Duncan, *Day by Day with J. B. Phillips* (Peabody, MA: Hendrickson Publishers, 2003), pages 234, 236.

9

Good News from Prejudiced Reporters

The Four Gospels

I T SEEMS NATURAL TO CALL THE BOOKS OF MATTHEW, MARK, LUKE, AND John biographies, since they tell us almost everything we know about the life of Jesus. But some students of literature are uncomfortable using the term *biography*, because these books don't approach the life of Jesus in a conventional way. Only two of them, Matthew and Luke, tell us anything about his birth; John chooses instead to give us an eternal view of Jesus' origins, then with a kind of astonishing casualness adds, "And the Word became flesh and lived among us" (John 1:14). Mark, on the other hand, worries himself not at all with early details of Jesus' life, bringing him on the scene at age thirty. But for that matter, all we know about Jesus' life from his birth until the beginning of his public ministry at age thirty is one incident that is recorded briefly but poignantly in Luke's Gospel (Luke 2:41-52).

All four books take us into the mind of Jesus through their extensive reports of his teaching, and all four tell us of his miracles—healing the sick, casting out demons, raising the dead. They also tell of his confrontations with the established religious leaders of his day, confrontations that eventually lead to his trial and crucifixion.

But above all they tell of Jesus' death. It is as if everything else in Jesus' story is primarily a prelude to his dying—and then, of course, his resurrection from the dead. This emphasis is especially clear in Luke's Gospel: "When the days drew near for him [Jesus] to be taken up, he set his face to go to Jerusalem" (Luke 9:51). The following chapters contain healings, conversations, parables, and other teaching, but always as complements to the big business, the destination in Jerusalem—where Jesus will die, as he several times reminds his disciples.

So yes, Matthew, Mark, Luke, and John are a different sort of biography. We might call them *biographies to a purpose*, because clearly enough they have in mind goals of their own. Mark opens with what has become a defining phrase: "The beginning of *the good news* of Jesus Christ" (Mark 1:1, emphasis added). *Gospel* means "good news," so when unknown persons centuries ago began titling these four books as "The Gospel According to [Matthew, Mark, Luke, John]," they were declaring that these books are, above all else, what Mark said: *good news*. They are good news for the human race and for our very planet—or, in the understanding of John and of the writers of the epistles, good news for the very universe and all its constituent parts.

I like to call the Gospels *campaign biographies*. Understand that I may be oversimplifying when I use this concept, but I think my approach will help us grasp something of the uniqueness of each Gospel and yet the dominant quality that pervades all four.

Here's what I mean. In those countries where free elections are held, elections are preceded by formal and informal biographies of the major candidates. In the United States these biographies take on fascinating variety, as the supporters of particular presidential candidates seek to win the votes of elements within the electorate. Thus business publications such as *Forbes, Fortune, BusinessWeek,* and *The Wall Street Journal* will examine the candidates in light of how their platform and personality will affect the economic community. A variety of Catholic publications and such Protestant periodicals as *The Christian Century* and *Christianity Today* will interpret the candidates' records for insight as to how they will respond to certain moral and ethical issues. So too with particular racial or ethnic groups: publications that are prepared especially for African-American, Hispanic, or Jewish readers will carry campaign biographies that emphasize issues that have special significance to these constituencies.

And so it was in the first century, when the Gospels were written. It seems rather clear that while the Gospels were available to any reader and of value to all, each one must have been especially persuasive to a particular element in the population. I will approach each of the Gospels with that format in mind. But before I do so, let me make two prefatory comments.

First, that my comparison is irregular at this point. The goal in contemporary campaign biographies is that a given candidate shall win votes from the specific constituencies, so that he or she can be elected. Not so with our Lord. He was already "elected." But by voting for him, persons elected themselves into his kingdom.

Second, let me underline the title of this chapter. Our reporters —call them Matthew, Mark, Luke, and John—are *prejudiced* reporters. They do not pretend to be objective. Mind you, they are dramatically honest—so honest that I suspect that many of us who preach and teach their words today may wish, at times, that they had been more selective in their reporting. But they are not objective. They believe in Jesus as their Lord, they have been utterly captured by him, and they want nothing more than to persuade their readers to the same discipleship. That's why we often refer to these four writers as *evangelists:* they want to convert us, to persuade us to follow the way they have chosen.

Matthew

As I have said before, it is generally agreed that Mark was the first Gospel written, but it is highly appropriate that Matthew is the first book in the New Testament, because Matthew so ably picks up the plot line from the Hebrew Scriptures. This is one of the reasons we're inclined to feel that this Gospel was written originally to appeal especially to the first-century Jewish audience.

See how this Gospel begins: "An account of the genealogy of Jesus the Messiah, the son of David, the son of Abraham" (Matthew 1:1). A genealogy—especially a bare-bones one—appeals to only a limited number. But for those first-century Jews who were waiting for a Messiah, a genealogy was the first issue. They may have had many expectations as to who and what the Messiah might be, but there was one absolute requirement: the Messiah had to have the right bloodline. He must be from the line of David and Abraham. Matthew gets this detail out of the way at the very beginning of his book, as if to say, "Now we can proceed with other matters."

And the matters with which he proceeds are directly tied to the Old Testament—including, for instance, a direct quotation in the line "Judah and his brothers" (Matthew 1:2; Genesis 44:14), a phrase that might seem incidental to a Gentile reader but that connected with the plot line for a first-century Jew. Then, still in this first chapter, we see a phrase that will appear often in this Gospel: "All this took place to fulfill what had been spoken by the Lord through the prophet" (Matthew 1:22). The Gospel writers all quote from the Hebrew Scriptures, but Matthew insists on underlining that he is doing so; he wants his intended audience to know that the events unfolding in the life of Jesus were already predicted by the Hebrew prophets. (See also, for example, Matthew 2:5; 2:17; 3:3; 12:17; 21:4.)

Then notice this line in chapter 1, as the writer concludes the genealogy: "So all the generations from Abraham to David are fourteen generations; and from David to the deportation to Babylon, fourteen generations; and from the deportation to Babylon to the Messiah, fourteen generations" (Matthew 1:17). To a postmodern reader this detail is only a numerical curiosity; we're likely to say, "So what?" Not so with Matthew's primary audience. The number seven was one of the especially significant numbers for students of the Hebrew Scriptures because it was the number of *completeness* (as in the Creation occupying seven days). But more than that, seven was a sacred number, as Robert Alter points out, so that the Hebrew word for *oath* (with its idea of covenant) seems to be derived from the sacred number of seven.[1] Matthew wants his readers to see that between these three crucial events in Israel's history there is always the identical number of generations: fourteen, the double multiple of seven.

And of course Matthew's Gospel emphasizes Jesus as the Teacher, a key theme to a people who revered knowledge. So this book brings together collections of teachings: for instance, the Sermon on the Mount (chapters 5 through 7), parables of the kingdom (chapter 13), and teachings on the end-times (chapters 24 and 25).

Notice, too, that while the other Gospel writers refer to the "kingdom of God," Matthew speaks of "the kingdom of heaven." Why? Because Jews were exceedingly careful about using the name of God, lest they be guilty of taking the name of God in vain, even if unintentionally. Apparently Matthew wants to respect this sense of reverence in his readers and hearers, so he substitutes the word *heaven*—much as a reverent person in our time might say, "For heaven's sake" where a less careful person would say, "For God's sake."

Mark

Mark seems to have aimed his campaign biography especially at the Romans. There's an interesting logic in this, of course, since tradition links Mark's Gospel with his mentor, Peter, and with teachings Mark received from the apostle while with him in Rome.

The style of this Gospel surely fits the first-century Romans. They were the world's premier administrators; still today a traveler in either continental Europe or the British Isles will be shown roads and aqueducts and walls that were erected by the Romans as they established their remarkable empire.

So what would Romans look for in a religious leader? They wouldn't care about genealogies; and while they would be interested in the leader's philosophy, as conveyed by his teachings, they would find something else far more crucial. Quite simply the Romans would ask, "Can he bring it off?" They looked for strength, decisiveness, the ability to deal with crises; they looked, that is, for a take-charge type of personality.

Unlike Matthew and Luke, therefore, Mark's Gospel doesn't begin with a birth story. Instead the author brings us into Jesus' life when our Lord is thirty years old, introducing us to Jesus by way of John the Baptist, who might well be called Jesus' advance agent. "As it is written in the prophet Isaiah, 'See, I am sending my messenger ahead of you, / who will prepare your way; / the voice of one crying out in the wilderness: / "Prepare the way of the Lord, / make his paths straight"'" (Mark 1:2-3). Mark then gives us a succinct paragraph about John the Baptist and his ministry, leading immediately into the story of John's baptizing Jesus and of the divine endorsement that accompanied the baptism.

Then, in the same breathless fashion, Mark tells us that Jesus was driven into the wilderness for forty days, where he was "tempted by Satan," and that "after John was arrested, Jesus came to Galilee, proclaiming the good news of God" (Mark 1:13, 14). Then, before the forty-five brief verses of the first chapter end, Mark also reports on Jesus' enlisting his first disciples, healing a man with an unclean spirit, healing a number of persons at Simon's house, embarking on a preaching mission throughout Galilee, and cleansing a leper. And if it seems to you that this is a great deal to pack into a chapter of roughly a page-and-a-half in average type, you won't be surprised to hear that the favorite word in Mark's Gospel is a Greek word, *euthus*, which is translated as "immediately," "straightway," "at once," or whatever word or phrase a translator can find to communicate business that brooks no delay. As Eugene Peterson puts it: "There's an air of breathless excitement in nearly every sentence" Mark writes.[2]

One thing is very clear: the author of this Gospel is in a hurry. This could be explained on the ground that it was the first Gospel written and is therefore a kind of brief, summary story; but in truth, while Mark is likely the first Gospel of the four in our New Testament, we don't by any means know that it was the first written. I choose rather to feel that the author knows the readership for which he is writing. The Romans are a people in a hurry. They have an empire to run. If they are to hear a story, the story had better come to them in the direct, here-are-the-facts fashion of a communiqué to a military officer or to a chief executive from one of his advisors.

This Gospel is a book of action, no doubt about it. The Bible before me has thirty-four pages for Matthew, thirty-six pages for Luke, and just twenty-two for Mark, but they all tell essentially the same story. Indeed, that's why they're called the *synoptic* Gospels, because they see the story with the "same eye." But Mark condenses the teaching portions that have so much prominence in Matthew's account, and he has no genealogies, and of course no birth-story. The occasional instances where Mark elaborates are in his accounts of miracles. Because the miracles represent action; they show Jesus' authority and power, and that's the kind of mood Mark wants to emphasize. And I should add that along with *immediately,* Mark's other favorite word is *authority.* Jesus knew how to get things done.

GOOD NEWS FROM PREJUDICED REPORTERS

Luke

If, as tradition says, this Gospel was written by Luke the physician, who also gave us the Book of Acts, its author is the only Gentile among the New Testament writers. The prologue to his Gospel reflects his Greek upbringing, and his Gospel as a whole has a style very much its own. As surely as Mark's Gospel seems aimed at a Roman audience, Luke's seems aimed at the Greeks.

Having said that, though, I'm sure there were first-century Greeks with whom Mark's style resonated, and I'm equally sure there were first-century Romans who were most at home with Luke's approach. That is, ethnic or cultural distinctions in taste are tendencies or learnings, not inviolable categories.

Luke is the poet, the artist, the gentle, sensitive man. Since the fourteenth century, he has been the patron saint of painters. Ancient tradition says that he himself did a portrait of Mary, the mother of Jesus. Since the late second century, Luke has been identified as the "beloved physician" who traveled with Paul, so that Jerome would write in the early fifth century that "as often as his [Luke's] book is read in the Church, so often does his medicine flow out."[3]

Luke promises as he begins his story that he is going to give "an orderly account." But orderly is in the eye of the beholder; I doubt that Mark would have seen Luke's way as orderly. Because Luke begins, not with a genealogy, as Matthew's logic would demand, and not with action, as Mark wants, but with a human-interest story. He begins the way a master storyteller would, giving us the fascinating background events prior to the birth of John the Baptist. Luke wants us to know that John the Baptist, the forerunner of Jesus, is himself a miracle.

And Luke gives us poetry. He is the only Gospel writer to include Zechariah's song (*Benedictus*) (1:59-79), Mary's song (*Magnificat*) (1:46-55), the song of the angels (*Gloria in Excelsis Deo*) (2:14), and Simeon's song (*Nunc dimittis*) (2:29-32). Luke's idea of orderly leaves room for poetry; indeed, poetry gets what we would call prime time. The Greeks, with their love of beauty, would love Luke's approach—as would any other reader who is drawn to the artistic.

Luke was surely a very learned man, but he also possessed particular affection for the lost, the lonely, the disinherited, and the outsiders. The Bible as a whole has a heart for such, but Luke wears his heart on his sleeve. When he tells the birth story, he features the shepherds in a special vignette in spite of their despised occupation. When Joseph and Mary present Jesus at the temple, it is with the poor people's offering (Luke 2:24; see Leviticus 12:8). It is Luke who includes the story of the rich man and Lazarus (16:19-31), where the rich man is anonymous and the beggar has a name. Luke tells us of the conversion of Zacchaeus, with Jesus' magnificent words, "For the Son of Man came to seek out and to save the lost" (19:10). And of course it is Luke who tells us of the conversion of the dying thief (23:39-43). Is it because Luke is himself an outsider, a Gentile, or is it simply that he is someone of a great heart, a person with a kind of universal citizenship? Who can say?

John

As I mentioned earlier, we speak of the first three Gospels as synoptic, because in large part they tell the same story with the same basic emphasis. It is only in the kinds of specifics that I've been listing that differences appear. John, however, has his own story to tell and his own dramatic way of telling it.

In my little formula of the Gospels as campaign biographies, I have described Matthew as appealing especially to the Jewish reader, Mark to the Roman, and Luke to the Greek. John seems to me to be written for the Christian; it is a biography for the party members, to add to their enthusiasm and loyalty.

This Gospel is difficult to accept unless one is a convinced believer. It begins with a voice from every instrument in the orchestra and every person in the chorus, telling us that Jesus was from "the beginning," and that "all things came into being through him, and without him not one thing came into being" (John 1:1, 3). Where Matthew begins the story with a genealogy, Mark with the beginning of Jesus' ministry, and Luke with the birth of Jesus' forerunner (John the Baptist), John goes back beyond the reaches of history, to tell us that Jesus was "with God" and "was God."

And where the other Gospels wait until rather far into Jesus' ministry for Peter's declaration that Jesus was the Messiah sent from God, already in the first chapter of this Gospel John the Baptist identifies Jesus as "the Son of God" (1:34); and Andrew, Philip, and Nathanael in quick succession declare Jesus to be the Messiah (1:41), the one of whom Moses wrote (1:45), and the Son of God, the King of Israel (1:49).

All of which is to say that John's Gospel is not for the faint of heart. Nor does Jesus make it any easier when he refers to himself. He tells the woman of Samaria that he is the Messiah (4:25-26). When some religious leaders question his healing on the Sabbath, Jesus replies that anyone who hears his voice and believes him "has eternal life" (5:24). Later he tells another gathering that he is "the bread of life," and that "those who eat my flesh and drink my blood have eternal life, and I will raise them up on the last day" (6:48, 54). And on the last day of a festival, Jesus throws out a challenge to the crowd: "Let anyone who is thirsty come to me, and let the one who believes in me drink. As the scripture has said, 'Out of the believer's heart shall flow rivers of living water'" (7:37-38). And so it continues, one crescendo after another, through the Gospel of John. And when the writer comes to the end of his account he says with beautiful frustration, "But there are also many other things that Jesus did; if every one of them were written down, I suppose that the world itself could not contain the books that would be written" (21:25).

But this author knows why he has written what he has. It is "so that you may come to believe that Jesus is the Messiah, the Son of God, and that through believing you may have life in his name" (20:31).

The writers of the four Gospels were on to something—something they were utterly certain of and knew to be magnificently eternal. None of the authors identified themselves by name; the names were attached by tradition in the next few generations after the Gospels were written. The test, as Luke defined it, was that the authors had to have been firsthand witnesses or persons who had gotten the story from eyewitnesses. They were evangelists, passionate about getting out the vote for Jesus so that those who accepted him as their Lord might enter into the same eternal life that these writers themselves had experienced. They couldn't wait to tell the story.

---

[1] Robert Alter, *The Five Books of Moses* (New York: W. W. Norton & Company, 2004), pages 106, ff.

[2] Eugene H. Peterson, *The Message* (Colorado Springs: Navpress, 1993), page 74.

[3] Maisie Ward, *They Saw His Glory* (New York: Sheed and Ward, 1956), page 129.

10

The Church Is Born

The Acts of the Apostles

Anyone who professes to be a Christian should spend a lot of time in the book of Acts. At first I was going to say, "Anyone who professes to be a Christian will love the book of Acts," but then I realized that this is definitely not guaranteed. Some who profess to be Christians think of their religion as a private affair, so they pride themselves somewhat on not belonging to a church; such persons won't enjoy Acts, because this book makes it very clear that Christianity is a community affair. Like it or not, we become part of a community when we take Christ as Lord, and if we absent ourselves from this body we do so in violation of what it means to be part of "the body of Christ." Some other believers will find Acts upsetting for a quite different reason. These are the people who have a very idealistic view of the church; they know that the church they belong to isn't perfect, so they long for the truly good old days, the Early Church, when things were as they ought to be. But when these people read the book of Acts, they are baptized in reality: the first believers were a wonderfully, pathetically human lot. They not only made mistakes, they made them in boldfaced type, *fortissimo.*

And of course it is for the information I've just given that we need to read the Acts of the Apostles. We need to know what the church was like in its earliest days in order to disabuse ourselves of any comfortable illusions, and to compel us to take our place with the continuing body of Christ. We need to know how human the church has always been so that we will not give up on the church as we sometimes experience it, but we need, at the same time, to know the grand potential of the church so that we will never be content with the church as we experience it. And we need of course to know that

91

we are neither too good nor too bad to be part of this body. The better we are, the more the church needs us; the worse we are, the more we need the church.

The book of Acts matters to us especially, however, because it is where you and I find our special role in the Eternal Plot. As you already know, every human being is in the plot from the very beginning, from Eden, because the Bible is the story of God's relationship with our whole human race. But for those of us who are Christians or who have some leanings in that direction—as is likely to be the case with most persons who have gotten this far in reading this Bible study—the book of Acts is where we see ourselves as among those helping to shape the plot. By definition Christians are among those who are working with God to bring the will of God to pass in the world.

What I mean is hinted at in the opening verse of the book of Acts, as presented in a number of translations, including the Revised Standard Version, the King James, and the New International Version. The person who wrote the third Gospel, the book of Luke, is also the author of the book of Acts, and he indicates that in Acts he is picking up the story that he began in the Gospel. "In the first book, O Theophilus, I have dealt with all that Jesus began to do and teach" (Acts 1:1 RSV). I'm struck by the word *began*. Obviously the author of Luke and Acts saw the two books as a continued story, and felt that these first believers were picking up the work that Jesus had begun. The New Testament describes Christians as "the body of Christ." The book of Acts makes one feel that Christ was still walking the streets of Jerusalem, and the roadways of Galilee and beyond. He had begun doing so in the Gospel story, and he was continuing to do so now through his followers.

But if Jesus Christ were to be such a living presence in the world, his followers would have to possess—and be possessed by—something quite beyond themselves. So it is that Jesus' last words to his followers as he ascended were a command that they "wait there for the promise of the Father," the infilling of the Holy Spirit, which would empower them to go to "the ends of the earth" (Acts 1:4, 8). Perhaps you've heard someone say that the Acts of the Apostles ought to be called, rather, the Acts of the Holy Spirit. This idea has merit, as the unfolding of the Acts soon makes clear.

THE CHURCH IS BORN

In the last year of Jesus' ministry, thousands came to hear him teach and preach and to observe his miracles. The description of Jesus' entry into Jerusalem on the day we now refer to as Palm Sunday indicates that many hundreds, perhaps an even larger number, hailed our Lord as their coming Redeemer. But Jesus' public trial and crucifixion winnowed out all but the most convinced. As a result, those who gathered in Jerusalem in obedience to Christ's command numbered only around 120. They "were constantly devoting themselves to prayer" (Acts 1:14), but they also took care of necessary church business—particularly, finding a successor to Judas, who had in anguish taken his own life after betraying Jesus.

On the day of Pentecost, a major Jewish feast day, the little group were all together in their upper room meeting place when "suddenly from heaven there came a sound like the rush of a violent wind, and it filled the entire house where they were sitting. Divided tongues, as of fire, appeared among them, and a tongue rested on each of them. All of them were filled with the Holy Spirit and began to speak in other languages, as the Spirit gave them ability" (Acts 2:2-4).

Even in the sparse, straightforward language of the biblical writer this sounds like a quite dramatic happening. But no one could have guessed just how dramatic and far-reaching it would be. This event is sometimes called the birthday of the church, because it is here that the worldwide, eternity-spanning institution of the church came into existence. Before this happening the handful of believers were a people with a calling but with no idea of how they would bring that calling to pass. Their leader had been crucified, and it seemed altogether possible that they might soon experience some similar fate. As a result, they were meeting rather much in secret. But within hours, 3,000 people joined their company of 120 (see Acts 2:41), and their fear was replaced by a boldness that made their spokesperson, Simon Peter, accuse the religious establishment of crucifying the one whom God had made "both Lord and Messiah" (Acts 2:36).

So however extraordinary the rushing wind, the tongues of fire, and the speaking in unlearned languages, something much more profound was at work. God had unloosed in the world a power that from that day forward would be the crucial deterrent to all that is evil, stagnant, destructive, and deadly on our planet. The Holy Spirit—that is, the very Spirit of God and of Christ—had come into the world, to dwell within and to empower all those who would allow themselves to be filled with God and to be used for God's purposes. In the nearly twenty centuries since then, it is to the degree that the church and its individual members have allowed the Holy Spirit to possess them that the will of God has been done in our world.

But of course this achievement was not then, nor has it ever been, without opposition. At first the story has a kind of idyllic quality. "Day by day" the believers "broke bread at home and ate their food with glad and generous hearts, praising God and having the good-will of all the people. And day by day the Lord added to their number those who were being saved" (Acts 2:46-47). On the one hand, this success led to opposition and the arrest of some of the leaders; and on the other hand the same success tempted some to the kind of hypocrisy that showed itself in the tragic story of Ananias and Sapphira (see Acts 5:1-11). And the lovely breaking of bread "with glad and generous hearts" was soon marred by feelings of jealousy, as one ethnic group felt the widows in their contingent were not treated as well as those in another (see Acts 6:1-2).

But good came out of even such potential trouble and dissension. Perhaps this is one of the significant evidences of the work of the Holy Spirit: not that there are no problems, but that the problems are transformed into progress. The apostles solved the divisive issue of the distribution of food by selecting "seven men of good standing, full of the Spirit and of wisdom" (Acts 6:3) to supervise the sharing of food; and behold, among the seven was a man called Stephen, who delivered the longest sermon recorded in the Acts, and who, in the process, became the first Christian martyr (see Acts 6:8–7:60); and another from the seven, Philip, became an instrument of evangelism in Samaria and then in a personal encounter with a strategic member of the Ethiopian government (see Acts 8:4-40).

As we read the Acts of the Apostles, we can easily miss the crucial points where the divine plot might have taken an unfortunate turn. If at the outset, for example, the apostles had failed to tarry in Jerusalem for the empowering by the Holy Spirit—well, I suspect there never would have been a book of Acts and there never would have been a church. It's at this point that we realize this book is, indeed, the Acts of the Holy Spirit, because without the Spirit's activity the story would have gone nowhere. And Peter and John's healing of the beggar who could not walk (see Acts 3) was a pivotal event, because with it the apostles learned that what Jesus had said was in fact true: the works Jesus had done, they were themselves now able to do (see John 14:12). Furthermore, it was this miracle that provided the platform from which Peter and John not only preached, but challenged the religious leadership of the nation (see Acts 3:11–4:12).

And as I have already indicated, when the apostles appointed seven persons (what we would now call *laypeople*) to supervise the distribution of the food, they set an impressive precedent and opened a door that must have surprised them even as they did it. The apostles recognized that no task in the church is minor, so they sought for persons who were "full of the Spirit and of wisdom"; the contemporary church would do well to have the same standards for greeters, ushers, choir members, worship leaders, trustees, and committee personnel. What the apostles probably did not expect is that these seven people who were appointed to do somewhat routine tasks would prove instead that they, too, had apostolic power. Indeed, the ministries of Phillip and Stephen seem to have been more memorable than those of some of the original Twelve. The apostles, working perhaps from the Old Testament pattern of a Levitical priesthood, may have been surprised to find that in the church the line between clergy and laity would not be so sharply defined—a lesson that the church has to relearn regularly.

Then there was the matter of church membership. This was an issue that had to be settled and defined several times. It happened first in Peter's encounter with Cornelius, "a centurion of the Italian Cohort ... a devout man who feared God with all his household" (Acts 10:1-2). But he was a Gentile, and at this point all the believers were Jews by either birth or conversion; that is, the first believers entered the door of the church by way of Judaism. But Peter's dramatic experience convinced him that "God shows no partiality, but in every nation anyone who fears him and does what is right is acceptable to him" (Acts 10:34-35).

The issue arose again when some unnamed leaders preached "to no one except Jews" in Phoenicia, Cyprus, and Antioch, yet some Gentiles were converted in Antioch. The church leaders sent Barnabas to evaluate the situation, and good man that he was, Barnabas rejoiced for the grace of God that he saw at work (Acts 11:19-26). But as Paul and Barnabas preached through a wide-ranging area, more and more Gentiles were converted, so that at last the leadership in Jerusalem had to make a formal decision: was belief in Christ enough, or must one also "be circumcised and ordered to keep the law of Moses" (Acts 15:5)? Peter gave his witness, as did Barnabas and Paul. The council conferred, then declared, "For it has seemed good to the Holy Spirit and to us to impose on you no further burden than these essentials: that you abstain from what has been sacrificed to idols and from blood and from what is strangled and from fornication. If you keep yourselves from these, you will do well" (Acts 15:28-29).

By this decision, believers in Jesus Christ ceased to be a branch of Judaism. I doubt that the council realized how far-reaching their decision was going to be. But it was a prayerful decision, guided by the Holy Spirit, and multitudes around the world in the succeeding centuries have profound reason to be grateful for it.

But as far as the latter half of the book of Acts is concerned, no event may have played a greater part in shaping the church than the one that began as a kind of footnote to the martyrdom of Stephen. As Stephen died with a prayer for forgiveness for his killers, the author of Acts adds, simply, "And Saul approved of their killing him" (Acts 8:1). This is our introduction to the person who will come to be known as the apostle Paul, the first great missionary of the church and arguably its most strategic theologian. Every theologian since the first century has built upon or argued with the apostle Paul. You can love him or not, but you can't ignore him.

Paul came into his faith in Christ through the back door. When he describes himself as "one untimely born ... the least of the apostles, unfit to be called an apostle," he's not speaking with mock humility. He knows who he is and what he has done, and the cloud of it pursues him, "Because I persecuted the church of God" (1 Corinthians 15:8-9). Christ confronted him when he was "breathing threats and murder against the disciples of the Lord," when he was so driven by his passion to destroy the movement that he had gotten authorization to go all the way to Damascus to hunt out believers and "bring them bound to Jerusalem" (Acts 9:1-2). His conversion was dramatic. I suspect nothing less would have worked for this man who was so fanatically set on his mission of destruction.

Ironically, Paul's conversion was so miraculous that many in the church couldn't believe it. His testimony and his scholarship "confounded the Jews who lived in Damascus by proving that Jesus was the Messiah," but when he went to Jerusalem, to be near the revered leaders of the church, "they were all afraid of him, for they did not believe that he was a disciple" (Acts 9:22, 26). If it hadn't been for that transparently good man Barnabas, one wonders what would have happened to Paul. (See Acts 9:27-28.)

And he remained controversial (indeed, some would add, to this very day). He saw himself as called particularly to the Gentiles, and when it seemed to him that Simon Peter (Cephas) was not being forthright in the issue, he confronted him "before them all" (Galatians 2:14). Some questioned Paul's apostleship; Paul responded that his converts were the best proof that he was an apostle (see 1 Corinthians 9:1-2). He confessed during one of his periods of imprisonment that some were hoping by their preaching to "increase my suffering in my imprisonment." This bothered him not at all. "What does it matter," he answered, as long as "Christ is proclaimed in every way" (Philippians 1:17-18).

This was Paul's passion, no doubt about it: that Christ should be proclaimed. He went on missionary expeditions. First with Barnabas, then Silas, and later with several others, especially Timothy. Paul was not the first to preach to the Gentiles, but he was the one who recognized that they were his special responsibility—a responsibility that took on unique significance after he received a vision in which a man of Macedonia pleaded with him, "Come over to Macedonia and help us." Paul and his team "immediately tried to cross over to Macedonia, being convinced that God had called us to proclaim the good news to them" (Acts 16:9-10).

According to his own testimony, Paul was not an eloquent preacher, though his preaching must surely have had remarkable power, else he wouldn't have had so many converts in so many places—nor would he have engendered so much opposition. But we know him today primarily for his letters. We shall say more about them in another chapter, but let it simply be said at this point that Paul's letters translated the good news of Christ into a coherent body of beliefs.

In the Bible that is before me just now, the Acts of the Apostles numbers thirty-three pages, and fully twenty of them have to do primarily with Paul, his conversion and his ministry. Which is to say that some forty percent of this book tells the acts of the apostles, and the other sixty percent the acts of one particular apostle, Paul. This is all the more remarkable since a body of people throughout Paul's ministry questioned his apostleship, since he had not been with Jesus during our Lord's earthly ministry.

And for that very reason you and I may feel especially close to the man of Tarsus. Like us, he came to know Jesus Christ by faith rather than by sight. It seems wonderfully appropriate that the book of Acts begins with people who had known Jesus firsthand: the eleven apostles, the faithful women, and Judas's successor, Matthias—a person who qualified for consideration because he was one of those who had been part of Jesus' ministry "beginning from the baptism of John until the day when he was taken up from us" (Acts 1:21-22), but that the book is then taken over by a latecomer, Saul of Tarsus.

And we other latecomers are still joining the team, nearly twenty centuries later.

11

Letters to New Believers

Romans Through Thessalonians

LET ME TELL YOU SOMETHING QUITE STRANGE AND WONDERFUL ABOUT the New Testament. Its oldest portion—and in some ways its most important—is made up of *letters.*

This is strange, because we don't instinctively think of letters when we discuss literature; we think of history, philosophy, stories, and poetry. Mind you, letters have had their place. In the first century B.C., Atticus and Tiro published almost a thousand of Cicero's letters, and through some periods of history certain writers raised letter writing to a level of elegance. The collected letters of major political figures such as Abraham Lincoln and Winston Churchill are widely read by students of history, as are the letters of such literary figures as Charles Dickens, Robert Louis Stevenson, Thomas Wolfe, and C. S. Lewis.

But I submit that no letters have been more widely circulated and more carefully analyzed than those of a first-century missionary and theologian, the apostle Paul, and certainly no one else's letters have been translated into as many different languages. Paul wrote these letters as highly personal documents to little bodies of people, often so small that it seems presumptuous to call them congregations, though I can't think of a better name. And because the letters are so personal in style and content, when we read them we sometimes have the feeling that we are looking over someone's shoulder, reading their correspondence—which, in a very real sense, is the case. That's part of the wonderful element in these letters. Still more wonderful, as we read we often realize that although Paul and the other authors didn't know us and couldn't have imagined the modern world, their letters fit our lives as if they were originally intended for us.

And although these letters were originally addressed to specific congregations or individuals, they very shortly went into wider publication. Not, of course, in the way we use that term nowadays. The method of reproduction was altogether primitive: any additional copies had to be made by hand. But because the letters meant so much, someone was always ready to make a copy for someone else. In our day, *copyright* means to protect the rights of the author from illegal use of his or her materials. In the first-century world, *copy right* meant, for all practical purposes, "Don't make any mistakes in what Paul (or Peter, or John, or James) wrote."

We can easily—and correctly, I think—imagine what happened when someone received a letter from an apostolic leader. The word spread rapidly, as someone might travel to the next community. Christians in one group were anxious—proud, no doubt—to share their letter with another body, in another city. And while some of the information in some of the letters (I think especially of Paul's letters to the people at Corinth) was not complimentary to the persons to whom the letter was originally addressed, there was apparently no hesitation in letting others see it. Probably the shortcomings of any group were more than likely to be found in the next group as well, so no one felt superior to a group in question.

It is this very quality of immediacy and transparency that makes these letters not only so authentic but also so valuable. They are vivid pictures of life and people in the first generation of the church, and there is no question but that the pictures are "warts and all." When Paul complains that he cannot speak to the Corinthian congregation "as spiritual people, but rather as people of the flesh, as infants in Christ," we know how disappointed he feels. But when he tells them a few hundred words later that they are "God's temple and that God's Spirit dwells in" them, we know his expectations were high (1 Corinthians 3:1, 16). We know that these first Christians had to cope with sexual immorality (1 Corinthians 5:1), jealousy over roles of ministry (1 Corinthians 12:4-11), false doctrine (Galatians 1:6-10), and disagreements between the apostles (Galatians 2:11-14).

But it is in this dramatically human setting of sins, problems, confusions, misunderstandings, and frustrations that some of the most beautiful and important writing of the centuries came into being. I venture that no short essay in any language is more cherished and more widely and frequently read than the thirteenth chapter of First Corinthians, Paul's discourse on love. But Paul wasn't writing an essay. He was simply trying to help a little group of Christians understand that no spiritual gift they might exercise, whether tongues, prophecy, wisdom, or healing, was as important as Christian love— *agape*, to use the Greek word that Paul employed.

And then there is the majestic statement of doctrine in Paul's letter to the people at Philippi, in which he says of Christ Jesus,

> Who, though he was in the form of God,
>   did not regard equality with God
>   as something to be exploited,
> but emptied himself,
>   taking the form of a slave,
>   being born in human likeness.
> And being found in human form,
>   he humbled himself
>   and became obedient to the point of death—
>   even death on a cross.

> Therefore God also highly exalted him
>   and gave him the name
>   that is above every name,
> so that at the name of Jesus
>   every knee should bend,
>   in heaven and on earth and under the earth,
> and every tongue should confess
>   that Jesus Christ is Lord,
>   to the glory of God the Father. (Philippians 2:6-11)

These verses (some see them as a first-century hymn that Paul was quoting, and others as poetry Paul himself wrote) describe the Incarnation, in which Christ "emptied himself" of his divinity in order to come to earth "in human form" and suffer death by crucifixion. But as Paul wrote it, he wasn't seeking to make a doctrinal statement. He was hoping simply to exhort his Philippian believers to work together with humility, looking not to their own interests but to the interests of others (see 2:4).

And here is some of the great beauty and strength of these letters and of their teaching of doctrine. They present doctrine not as a separate study, but as part of the believers' daily lives; indeed, Paul seems sometimes to bring in doctrine almost incidentally and certainly in a very natural, pragmatic way. This approach surely corrects our contemporary attitude that often sees doctrine as a study for those who "have the time" to pursue it or who are interested in such specialized matters. Paul treats doctrine in very matter-of-fact fashion, as part of the data of daily living. The major exceptions are in his letter to the Galatians, where he is dealing with the importance of the Crucifixion, and in his letter to the Romans, where he puts some of his teachings in a more structured form for a congregation he has not yet visited.

So let us begin our short references to Paul's letters with the **Letter to the Romans.** This book is the first in the New Testament collection of the Epistles, probably because it is the longest of the letters. But if those who organized the books of the New Testament were arranging the letters by their importance, a case could surely be made for Romans to lead the way. Written probably in the spring of A.D. 57, it is Paul's most sustained doctrinal statement. He begins by declaring that the knowledge of God is available to the whole human race because "ever since the creation of the world" God's power and nature have been revealed "through the things he has made," so that we are "without excuse" (Romans 1:20). But we are all sinners: "all, both Jews and Greeks [Gentiles]" (Romans 3:9). The Jews have an advantage in their having received the Law of Moses, but the Law cannot save, it can only reveal our sinfulness.

Our hope is this, that "while we were still weak, at the right time Christ died for the ungodly" (5:6). But even with grace, we humans have a struggle. Paul speaks for himself, but honest souls will take their stand with him when he writes, "So I find it to be a law that when I want to do what is good, evil lies close at hand" (7:21). In the midst of such a dilemma Paul rejoices in the deliverance promised "through Jesus Christ our Lord" (7:25). Paul goes on to explain (in what is both a doctrinal declaration and a devotional witness) life in the Spirit. He pledges his undying loyalty to his people, the Jews, though he feels they have temporarily rejected the way of grace.

Then, in a style that we will see repeatedly in the letters, he moves into practical issues of the day by day living out of the Christian life.

If Romans is a book of theology, **First and Second Corinthians** are fascinating studies in how to deal with frustrating problems in a difficult congregation. These books are also our most revealing insight into the personality of the great apostle. The Corinthians don't appreciate Paul as much as they should (partly, I'm sure, because they don't understand him as they should), so Paul defends himself and in the process lets us into his heart. The congregation is divided by their loyalties to the several preachers and teachers who have led them; there is sexual immorality within the membership, and lawsuits between believers; the people argue with one another over who is the most spiritual; they show preferential attitudes at—of all times!—the celebration of the Lord's Supper; some are confused about a key doctrine of their new faith, the resurrection of the dead. And all of this is only in the first letter!

But Paul is a magnificent optimist: "Since it is by God's mercy that we are engaged in this ministry," he writes, "we do not lose heart" (2 Corinthians 4:1). And he has reason for his optimism: the churches of Macedonia, learning of the desperate need of the church in Jerusalem, had sent an offering: "Their abundant joy and their extreme poverty have overflowed in a wealth of generosity" (2 Corinthians 8:2). Now Paul appeals to the Corinthians to respond in the same fashion. I repeat, Paul is an optimist, a holy optimist. He concludes this letter— one, again, in which he has had to deal with severe issues—"This is what we pray for, that you may become perfect" (2 Corinthians 13:9). This is what Paul expected Christians to be. Perfect. Simple, isn't it?

Well, not really. We learn how difficult it is when we read the **Letter to the Galatians**—a letter written in such white heat that Paul skips all courteous formalities with an in-your-face, "Paul an apostle—sent neither by human commission nor from human authorities, but through Jesus Christ and God the Father" (Galatians 1:1). False believers, as Paul so sharply puts it, have come to the churches of Galatia insisting that Gentile believers must be circumcised and fulfill other elements of the Mosaic Law if they are to be saved.

Paul, who before his conversion had been the most zealous in advocating the Jewish law, is now the most vehement in declaring that Christ's death on the cross is enough: "For if justification comes through the law, then Christ died for nothing" (Galatians 2:21). This epistle was a key factor in Martin Luther's spiritual pilgrimage; he said that he was married to it.[1] Its message continues to be as pertinent in the twenty-first century as in the first. There is always a tendency for believers to try to supplement the grace of God, as if the work of Christ were not enough.

The **Letter to the Ephesians** introduces us to the language of teaching that is at the same time the language of devotion. In this letter the apostle seems at times unable to contain the grandeur of the faith he is experiencing. For example, verses three through fourteen in chapter 1 are just one sentence in the Greek, as if Paul can't find a point of closure. He employs all sorts of superlative language: "before the foundation of the world" (1:4), "grace ... lavished on us" (1:7-8), "the fullness of time" (1:10), "the immeasurable greatness of his power for us who believe" (1:19), to name just a few. At times Paul seems to struggle to find language that is extravagant enough for his purposes.

The focus of all this extravagant purpose of God is in us, in day-by-day believers, so that we "may be filled with all the fullness of God" (Ephesians 3:19). God's power is "at work within us ... to accomplish abundantly far more than all we can ask or imagine" (3:20). Several things strike me as I read such things. First, that Paul was writing originally to quite ordinary persons in Ephesus, most of them in the backwaters of culture and achievement. Then, I think of a recent chance conversation in an airport waiting area. "Preacher," this new acquaintance said, "my favorite Bible books are Psalms and Ephesians." As she spoke I understood her love for Psalms but was surprised to hear about Ephesians. Now, thinking of the people to whom Paul first wrote this book, I'm ashamed of my spiritual dullness. Also, I wonder why more of us aren't properly ecstatic about God's investment in us and the divine esteem in which we are held.

I expect that our problem is not simply an inability to grasp Paul's extravagant expectations in chapters 1 through 3, but also the very down-to-earth living out of our faith that he outlines in the three chapters that follow. When he writes, "I therefore, the prisoner in the Lord, beg you to lead a life worthy of the calling to which you have been called, with all humility and gentleness, with patience, bearing with one another in love" (4:1-2), we realize abruptly that we have come to, as the common phrase has it, where the rubber meets the road.

Now we are exhorted to "speak the truth to our neighbors," to "not let the sun go down" on our anger, to "work honestly with [our] own hands" (4:25-28). We're about to receive instructions on living as husbands and wives, parents and children, slaves and masters— and I doubt that these instructions were received any more kindly in Paul's day than they are today. I'm sure many of Paul's contemporaries saw him as a revolutionary while many today see him as an antiquated conservative. In truth he was seeking only to lead Christ's followers, whoever we may be, in paths of submissive love. But of course submissive love has never been a hot commodity.

You have probably heard the **Letter to the Philippians** referred to as Paul's letter of joy. Perhaps you've also heard that the people in Philippi were his favorite congregation. The first sentence is easier to prove than the second, perhaps largely because we love people and groups for particular reasons. We don't necessarily love one more than another, we just love them differently.

Paul writes this letter from prison. He is quick to assure the people at Philippi, however, that "what has happened to me has actually helped to spread the gospel" (Philippians 1:12). The guards know that he is imprisoned for Christ (which probably made it easier for Paul to witness to them), and somehow his imprisonment has made most of the brothers and sisters "speak the word with greater boldness and without fear" (1:14).

But Paul is "hard pressed" by one question, whether he hopes to "depart and be with Christ," which is "far better" for him, or to "remain in the flesh," which is better for those who need his ministry. He concludes that the second path is the right one for now. In any event, "living is Christ and dying is gain" (1:21-26). If we can ring in with Paul, we'll realize that we're always in a win-win situation.

There's a later indication, however, that Paul isn't yet ready to die, because he hasn't become all he believes God wants him to be. "I press on toward the goal for the prize of the heavenly call of God in

Christ Jesus" (3:14). His unrest is a matter of the spirit; as for his outward circumstances (the matters that ordinarily seem to bother us the most), he is at peace: "I have learned to be content with whatever I have" (4:11).

Paul's **Letter to the Colossians** always seems to me to have much in common with Ephesians in its style and its language. But Colossians is more vigorously theological, and it centers especially on the person of Jesus Christ. "He is the image of the invisible God, the firstborn of all creation; for in him all things in heaven and on earth were created, things visible and invisible, whether thrones or dominions or rulers or powers—all things have been created through him and for him" (Colossians 1:15-16). Paul portrays Christ in the same fashion as we find in the opening of the Gospel of John, as one who was from the beginning: "He himself is before all things, and in him all things hold together" (Colossians 1:17).

And if it seems to you that Paul is far removed from the Gospel story, he makes the tie in a quite dramatic way: "And through him [Jesus] God was pleased to reconcile to himself all things, whether on earth or in heaven, by making peace through the blood of his cross" (1:20). Ponder the extravagant contrast: the One who "is before all things" is the same one who dies on a criminal's cross for the salvation of humankind.

First and Second Thessalonians are almost surely the earliest of Paul's epistles (written in about A.D. 50) and thus the oldest portion of the New Testament. Paul wrote these letters to the believers in Thessalonica to deal with a number of concerns, and especially to answer their anxious questions about the return of Christ. In the first letter Paul reminded the people that Jesus' coming would be "like a thief in the night," but that this should not worry them because they were "not in darkness" and thus not to be surprised (1 Thessalonians 5:2-5). Nevertheless some of the believers continued to be troubled, and in the second letter Paul begs them "not to be quickly shaken in mind or alarmed ... that the day of the Lord is already here" (2 Thessalonians 2:2). There have been times in nearly every generation when people have felt that the return of Christ is near, but perhaps never more so than in the first century. This isn't surprising. It must have seemed very natural to those first believers that Jesus would return without delay, especially in light of the persecution many of them were enduring. They could easily sense the power of antichrist in the unfolding events of any given week. The struggle between good and evil that had marked the human story from the beginning was increasing in breadth and intensity. They must have reasoned that this struggle had now reached its climax and that the next step would have to be God's final intervention in the return of Jesus Christ.

But the battle was far from over. Indeed, looking back from our vantage point nearly two millennia later, it looks as if in the first century the conflict was only heating up to what was proving to be a very long war. As we read these first-century letters, our question is not so much, "When will Jesus return?" As it is, "How shall I fight the good fight until that day?"

---

[1] Roland Bainton, *Here I Stand* (Nashville: Abingdon Press, 1950), page 293.

12

Letters for the Next Generation

First Timothy Through Jude

I WISH WE COULD FILL IN MORE OF THE DETAILS AS OUR STORY MOVES from Paul to Timothy and Titus; from Peter to John Mark; or from cities like Antioch, Corinth, and Thessalonica to towns whose names are now completely lost to us. Or from Asia Minor and Macedonia to Spain and the British Isles in one direction, to India in another, or to North Africa, Egypt, and Ethiopia in still another.

Tradition and legends give us a delicate framework on which to build our own imaginings. We know from a story in the book of Acts that an official from the court of the Candace of Ethiopia was converted through a brief teaching interlude with Philip. Tradition says that this official carried the faith with him to his homeland, to establish what eventually became the Ethiopian Orthodox Church. Tradition also says that the apostle Thomas took the message to India, that Andrew went into part of what is now Russia, and that Matthew went to Persia and Parthia. Of course we think of Simon Peter going to Rome, and other traditions tell us that Thaddeus went to Armenia, that Nathanael to Phrygia, and that the latecomer to the Twelve, Matthias, went to Ethiopia and parts of Arabia.

But as I have already indicated, while these stories are part history, part tradition, and part legend, they would probably dim in comparison to the real stories of the largely unknown men and women who took the faith of Christ in every direction, fulfilling their Lord's command to go into all the world. Much of the early growth of the church must have come through persons who went from the first congregations in Philippi, Corinth, Thessalonica, or Athens to smaller cities nearby; and people from those secondary sites went then to still farther points. The most adventurous ones went to the far places, but massive penetration had to come through congregations that were nothing more than extensions of some mother church. And so the message spread, at times in the midst of fierce persecution and at times in periods of comparative if uneasy quiet; but always on and on.

The New Testament leads us into the second generation, via letters to Timothy and Titus. The three letters are often identified as the Pastoral Epistles, because they contain so much counsel to the young church leaders. We first meet Timothy when Paul finds him in Lystra—"the son of a Jewish woman who was a believer; but his father was a Greek" (Acts 16:1). Paul added Timothy to his small traveling team, and eventually we find his name in the letterhead, so to speak, of the Second Letter to the Corinthians as well as the first and second letters to the Thessalonians and the letters to Philippi and Colossae. Titus doesn't appear in the book of Acts, but we know from references in Second Corinthians and Galatians that he too traveled with Paul on occasion.

So it was that the transition began, from the first followers of Jesus to a new generation. But there are always perils in the passing of leadership in any movement. Students of political history often note that the liberals of one generation become the stand-patters of the second, and the reactionaries of the third. Indeed, one can find a pretty good study in seeing what happens to a family farm over several generations, or a small family business—or indeed, a closely held corporation. It's very difficult to maintain a dream, a vision, or a passion from one generation to another.

The letters known as **First Timothy, Second Timothy, and Titus** give us some insights into this process as it unfolded in the early Christian church. For centuries tradition credited these three letters to the apostle Paul. More recent scholarship has questioned whether Paul was actually the author—partly on the basis of the vocabulary in these letters compared to that which appears in such letters as Romans, Corinthians, Galatians, and so forth, and partly because the theology in these pastoral letters seems more developed, as if tuned to a later time. Others reason that these differences in language and ideas will naturally exist when one is dealing with different circumstances and subject matter. I suggest, on the one hand, that one never be too hasty to join forces with any given scholarly development, since such matters are always in a state of flux, and rightly so. At the same time, I like to feel that if it was not Paul himself who wrote these letters, it was someone close enough to Paul that he was writing either with Paul's authorization or in the mind and spirit of Paul. That is, I would be comfortable in thinking of these letters as being Paul's work, directly or indirectly, even though in many ways they have a different ring than some of the major epistles.

Paul has hardly finished his greeting in the First Letter to Timothy before he has launched into a warning about certain doctrines that are insinuating their way into the church: "Myths and endless genealogies that promote speculations rather than the divine training that is known by faith" (1 Timothy 1:4). Paul's goal is "love that comes from a pure heart, a good conscience, and sincere faith" (1:5). Who can argue with that? The only problem is in making it come to pass.

But it's when one goes from such sure generalities to details of daily life and conduct that the trouble sets in. The counsel regarding women's role in the church (2:8-15) offends many of us, and in truth it seems to contradict Paul's own practices. His cooperation in the ministry of Priscilla and Aquila, a wife and husband team (Acts 18:1-4, 18); his willingness when, in ministry with Silas, for the two of them to stay in the home of Lydia at Philippi, which obviously endorsed her place as a leader in that congregation (Acts 16:11-15, 40); and his staying in the house of Philip the evangelist, whose "four unmarried daughters ... had the gift of prophecy" (Acts 21:9), surely indicate Paul's acceptance of women's role of leadership in the church.

It is, however, the very nature of the letters to Timothy and Titus to deal with details. These details are not as exciting as the exalted statements about the nature of Christ in Ephesians and Colossians, nor are they as monumental as Paul's finely reasoned doctrinal statements in Romans. But they were matters that had to be dealt with, in a movement that was proceeding from house churches to some level of organization. In the early days Paul could say that God had ordained that "some would be apostles, some prophets, some evangelists, some pastors and teachers, to equip the saints for the work of ministry, for building up the body of Christ" (Ephesians 4:11-12). But the person who writes to Timothy and Titus is dealing with churches where there are bishops and deacons, so it is essential for the writer to say something about the qualifications for these offices and the persons who occupy them (1 Timothy 2:8-3:13; Titus 1:5-9).

One senses also while reading these pastoral letters that the church is indeed entering its second generation. Something of the exuberance, the what's-going-to-happen-next quality of the early chapters of Acts is no longer dominant. Instead the writer is pleading with the believers to "devote themselves to good works; these things are excellent and profitable to everyone" (Titus 3:8). There are instructions for older women, for younger men, for slaves and servants, for young widows, and for daily citizenship.

Something in my soul insists that one ought to be able to keep the excitement, awe, and fire of the first days of faith and revival as one moves into the routine business of committees and the ordinary paraphernalia of living. But it isn't easy, and some would say that it's impossible. Some might even say that it was never intended to be, that there is the ecstasy of first love and there is the honorable responsibility of translating that ecstasy into the ordinary tasks of daily life. I know that such persons have a point, but I wish the church might laugh more often, and that its plodding might more frequently include a few dance steps. And to be honest, I wish I saw more of that in the pastoral epistles.

Philemon is such an extraordinary little book. Some people simply miss it in their reading of the New Testament—after all, it's easy to slip by something of just a few hundred words—while others read it and wonder exactly why it is included in the sacred canon.

At the very least, Philemon is a prime example of how to write a gracious letter. In it the apostle Paul asks his friend, Philemon, to forgive Philemon's slave, Onesimus, for—it appears—running away and taking some money or possessions with him. It seems that in the meanwhile Onesimus has become a Christian through his association with Paul ("whose father I have become during my imprisonment" [Philemon 10]). So now, as Onesimus returns with Paul's letter of endorsement, he is to be received by Philemon "no longer as a slave but more than a slave, a beloved brother" (Philemon 16). John Knox, a distinguished twentieth-century New Testament scholar, sought to prove that this little book is included in the New Testament not simply as an intriguing insight into Paul as a friend to a man in peril, but because Onesimus may have played a key role in the formation of the New Testament. A man named Onesimus became Bishop of Ephesus late in the first century—and it was in Ephesus that most of Paul's letters were first collected and published. Perhaps, then, Paul's Letter to Philemon is included as Onesimus' "signature" (as Professor Knox puts it) to the collection.[1]

Hebrews is one of the most intriguing books in the New Testament. It is the only letter, other than First John, in which the author is not named. Also, unlike other letters, it doesn't begin with a greeting; instead it moves immediately into the subject matter, like a compelling essay—which, in a way, it is. It does conclude like a letter, however, in a few brief personal words and greetings.

But its big business is a vigorous appeal to some early converts to keep the faith. The letter—unlike most of Paul's epistles—is not addressed to a specific community. One judges that its original readers were Jewish converts to Christ; Paul lets us know as much by his opening words: "Long ago God spoke to our ancestors in many and various ways by the prophets" (Hebrews 1:1). The author makes his appeal throughout the letter by comparing the heroes and the teachings of the Hebrew Scriptures with the role of Jesus Christ. To tell you the truth, one can't appreciate the wonders of this book without a fairly good knowledge of the Old Testament.

The author begins by telling us that God has spoken "in these last days" by his Son (1:2). He then tells us that God's Son is superior to the angels—then interrupts himself to say that Jesus "is not ashamed to call [us] brothers and sisters" (2:11). Resuming his comparisons, he notes that Jesus is superior to Moses (a shocking idea to a Jew), because Moses was a servant of God while Jesus is the Son of God (see 3:1-6). So, too, Jesus was superior to the high priest. Again the author interrupts himself to tell us that in Jesus we have a high priest "who in every respect has been tested as we are, yet without sin"; for this reason we can "approach the throne of grace with boldness" (4:15-16).

But this blessing comes with a price: the aim is that we should "go on toward perfection" (6:1). And the writer is disappointed that the people he is addressing are "dull in understanding. For though by this time you ought to be teachers, you need someone to teach you again the basic elements of the oracles of God" (5:11-12). The writer builds to an impassioned appeal. The work of Christ has made any offering for sin unnecessary (10:18), therefore believers can with confidence "enter the sanctuary by the blood of Jesus" (10:19). Above all, the writer wants to be sure the faltering believers "are not among those who shrink back and so are lost," but rather are "among those who have faith and so are saved" (10:18, 39).

And with this he leads us into one of the most memorable portions of the New Testament, what we sometimes call the Faith Chapter or Faith's Hall of Fame. The author leads us through the stories of Abel, Noah, Abraham and Sarah, Isaac, Jacob, Joseph, Moses, and Rahab, with a quick summary of others ("time would fail me to tell") "of whom the world was not worthy" (11:32, 38). But having paraded before us this series of towering figures, here is the climax of it all: "Yet all these, though they were commended for their faith, did not receive what was promised, since God had provided something better so that they would not, apart from us, be made perfect" (11:39-40).

So what are we to do? We should "lay aside every weight and the sin that clings so closely, and run with perseverance the race that is set before us, looking to Jesus the pioneer and perfecter of our faith, who for the sake of the joy that was set before him endured the cross, disregarding its shame, and has taken his seat at the right hand of the throne of God" (12:1-2).

The writer of this anonymous letter is making the point (in much grander fashion) that I mentioned earlier: you and I are now part of the plot. The battle for goodness that began with Abel, the son of Adam and Eve, and that has included times when people paid for their faith with "mocking and flogging, and even chains and imprisonment" (11:36) is now entrusted to us. The writer of the letter to the Hebrews was afraid that the second generation of believers would let the cause slip. The same peril has marked the story of the church for nearly twenty centuries, but the people of faith have survived. And now it is our turn.

One might easily think that those unknown persons who established the order of our New Testament books were trying to make a point by having **The Letter of James** follow immediately after Hebrews, with its grand faith climax. Because although James deals with many subjects, we know him especially for the way he insists that God's people are known by their works, and that "faith by itself, if it has no works, is dead" (James 2:17).

In truth, there is no real disagreement between the two letters. James is simply insisting that faith that is all talk is no faith at all; faith authenticates itself by the conduct that follows. And of course it's interesting that James proves the importance of works with two of the same persons the book of Hebrews uses to demonstrate faith, Abraham and Rahab (see James 2:14-26). Whatever, the Letter of James is a no-nonsense document. It reads very much like one of the wisdom books of the Old Testament. Its 108 verses contain 54 commands, which means that the commands come in a rapid-fire style.

This letter is hard on the rich and on those who show favoritism to the rich. It reminds us that nothing in our anatomy is quite as dangerous as the tongue, that "small member" that "boasts of great exploits" (3:5). The writer warns against becoming too comfortable with the contemporary culture ("friendship with the world" [4:4]), and of boasting about tomorrow, since we "do not even know what tomorrow will bring" (4:14). But the letter encourages us to pray, no matter how inadequate we might seem to be, reminding us that the great Elijah "was a human being like us" (5:17). When I read this epistle I feel as if I am listening to my eighth-grade teacher telling me that I can do better than I'm doing, and that I'd better start to without delay.

The First Letter of Peter is often praised for the beauty of its writing, which has caused some scholars to question whether it could have been written by a Galilean fisherman like Peter. This argument in itself doesn't influence me against Peter; I remind myself that the president of the United States who left us with the most exquisite literature was Abraham Lincoln, who had less formal education than any of his predecessors or successors in the White House. This is because writing is partly a gift that is distributed in what appears to be haphazard fashion, but that is then nurtured by clear thinking and earnest labor.

This letter is addressed to "the exiles of the Dispersion" who are scattered over a rather wide area. This kind of language appears several times in the New Testament, reminding us that the first Christians were often being exiled from their original homes during periods of persecution. Of course those attempts to discourage believers had just the opposite effect: wherever they went, they took their faith with them. In our day, denominations and independent bodies send out missionaries by intention, but in the first century, government officials did so unintentionally.

Peter tells his readers that they have been blessed with something the prophets of old "made careful search and inquiry"; it is something "into which angels long to look" (1 Peter 1:10, 12). They have been "ransomed from the futile ways inherited from [their] ancestors" (1:18). So who are they now? They are "a chosen race, a royal priesthood, a holy nation, God's own people" (2:9). "Once you were not a people, / but now you are God's people; / once you had not received mercy, / but now you have received mercy" (2:10).

The shepherds and shopkeepers, slaves and day laborers, must have been encouraged by such extravagant language, even as they recognized that tomorrow they could lose everything because of their beliefs. It was no get-rich-quick gospel models were great that the believers might suffer for doing what was right. "Beloved, do not be surprised at the fiery ordeal that is taking place among you to test you, as though something strange were happening to you" (4:12). Our ancestors in the faith were a hardy bunch. They knew what they believed and in whom they believed, so they walked with confidence into the face of whatever future this world might hold.

The Second Letter of Peter warns against false doctrine, reminding readers that "we did not follow cleverly devised myths when we made known to you the power and coming of our Lord Jesus Christ, but we had been eyewitnesses of his majesty" (2 Peter 1:16). We will come upon this language again in John's first letter, and you will remember that Luke's Gospel insisted that those who told the story should be "those who from the beginning were eyewitnesses" (Luke 1:2). And, in the search for the person who would take Judas's place, they required that it should be "one of the men who have accompanied us during all the time that the Lord Jesus went in and out among us," who could "become a witness with us to his [Jesus'] resurrection" (Acts 1:21-22). We can be impressed that the earliest Christians insisted on the integrity of their message and they knew that from a human point of view it depended on their apostolic memory.

The First Letter of John begins without identifying the author and without the formality of a greeting. It's as if the writer can't wait to make his point. No Christian doctrine is more crucial than the belief in Jesus Christ, as declared in the language of the ancient Nicene Creed, that he is "of one Being with the Father" and yet he "became truly human." People in our twenty-first century tend to have more trouble believing that Jesus Christ is "of one Being with the Father"; false teachers in the first century denied that Jesus "became truly human." They wouldn't accept that God had come to our planet in a physical, mortal body.

This teaching is known as the Gnostic heresy; it has continued to reappear over the centuries in one form or another—a heresy that claims to have special, "inside" knowledge that ordinary believers do not have. So the writer throws out his vigorous challenge: "We declare to you what was from the beginning, what we have heard, what we have seen with our eyes, what we have looked at and touched with our hands, concerning the word of life" (1 John 1:1). And when, later in the letter, the apostle explains how believers can know whether a spirit is from God, he returns to this test: "By this you know the Spirit of God: every spirit that confesses that Jesus Christ has come in the flesh is from God, and every spirit that does not confess Jesus is not from God" (4:2).

But though the writer is so emphatic in his appeal for doctrinal integrity in this letter, his major appeal is for living out the faith: one cannot claim to be living in the light "while hating a brother or sister" (2:9). "For this is the message you have heard from the beginning, that we should love one another" (3:11).

I am impressed that as the church entered its second generation, near the end of the first century, it did so with a balanced message: know the truth and live the life. We fool ourselves if we think we can separate the knowing and the living, the doctrine and the

117

performance. But of course we don't plan to separate them; when it happens, it is not by planning but by unconscious neglect.

The Second Letter of John deals again with the false teaching that Jesus only *seemed* to come in the flesh; any person who so teaches is "the deceiver and the antichrist" (2 John 7). **The Third Letter of John** is a kind of housekeeping letter, urging a man named Gaius to continue offering hospitality to itinerant teachers and warning against the influence of Diotrephes, "who likes to put himself first," while commending Demetrius, about whom "everyone has testified favorably" (3 John 9, 12).

The Letter of Jude is an impassioned appeal for its readers "to contend for the faith that was once for all entrusted to the saints" (Jude 3). Jude's language is vigorous, his figures of speech dramatic, and his warnings unrelenting. He concludes with a blessing that is appropriate to the mood and concerns of his letter: "Now to him who is able to keep you from falling, and to make you stand without blemish in the presence of his glory with rejoicing, to the only God our Savior, through Jesus Christ our Lord, be glory, majesty, power, and authority, before all time and now and forever. Amen" (Jude 24-25).

These letters from the first-century church sound to me like battle documents from the front lines of the conflict. The first Christians are thoroughly outnumbered. They have virtually no one of power or influence within their ranks. The Roman Empire says that you can worship as you like, as long as you remember also to worship the emperor. Both the Christians and the Jews refuse to worship the emperor, but the Christians make it still worse for themselves by being an evangelistic body that seeks to win others to their point of view.

If God's plot was to work in those first generations through such a body as the church, the plot surely seems in peril. But someone has said that Christianity survived because it outlived, out-thought, out-loved and out-died its enemies. I suspect that is why people around the world are still reading letters written by relatively unknown teachers and preachers to even more anonymous followers, while the letters of kings and emperors from that century are part of the dust.

---

[1]John Knox, "The Epistle to Philemon," in vol. 11 of *The Interpreter's Bible*, ed. George Arthur Buttrick, (Nashville: Abingdon Press, 1955), page 560.

13

The Curtain Falls, but the Drama Has Just Begun

The Book of Revelation

So IS THE GRAND PLOT COMING TO ITS END? YES AND NO. THE BOOK
of Revelation tells us in dramatic and sometimes exotic language
how one phase of the story will consummate, but only as a way of
leading us into the next chapter. And the next chapter is unending.

This, of course, is an appropriate way for our plot to end. It's the
only proper way, since from Genesis, chapter 1, this story has been
acted out on two stages, earth and heaven. Or to put it another way,
if this were a drama being performed in a theater, the playbill would
have a line for each act, identifying the *time* of the action. But
because of the nature of this story, it would be necessary always to
identify two times, God's and ours. Thus Genesis might have this
entry: time: *Human*—the beginning; *Divine*—unmeasured. Or find
yourself a better word if you will. You get the idea.

Henry Sloane Coffin, one of the great preacher-educators of the
first half of the twentieth century, put it this way: "But no attempt to
give the Bible's view of history dare ignore the perspective in which
that history is set. Its goal is not in history, but beyond it." He goes
on to say that the Christian church had very small beginnings and a
checkered history throughout, but "Christians early learned not to
look for the completion of their hopes at any time on earth."[1]

For this reason, Christians have always needed some insights into
the end of the story. This is not because Christians are weaker than
other people. As a matter of fact, from what we know, humans have
always wanted to know what is *beyond,* where the story is going to

end. This is one of the finest attributes of our humanness: we believe there is more to us individually than a bone and a hank of hair that will disintegrate into dust, and more to us corporately than a meaningless and purposeless more-of-the-same, more-of-the-same. We believe there is a plot and that we are part of it, however small our role may be.

We find that plot in the Bible, and the plot comes to its grand climax in the book of Revelation. The book of Revelation was written by a man named John, sometime late in the first century, probably between A.D. 69 and 96. In other words, it was written while the church was still very young, only a little ways into its second generation. It's possible, in fact, that its first readers could have included some persons who had been children or teenagers at the time of the crucifixion and resurrection of our Lord. We can't identify definitely the author of this book since John was a fairly common name in the first century, and since four persons by that name are mentioned in the New Testament. Professor Bruce M. Metzger notes that since no other identification is given (such as "John Mark" or "John the Elder") we can conclude that the author of Revelation was so well known that no other title or credential was needed.[2] Beginning in the mid-second century, the apostle John was commonly looked upon as the author. No matter, the authority of the book speaks for itself.

Since Revelation was written late in the first century, it was written following the brutal persecution by Nero and the increasingly severe restrictions of Emperor Domitian. The book promises believers that God is still supreme and that heaven's victory is assured, though there may be great suffering before that blessed consummation. John wrote Revelation while in banishment on the Isle of Patmos, where the Roman government often sent political prisoners. His imprisonment there may indicate the feeling of the government that the Christians were a threat to the government. The fact that Christians would not recognize Domitian as a god or worship him was offense enough, and their continuing growth in the face of opposition made them seem all the more threatening, even though they had no army and very few persons of power or influence.

All the books of the New Testament show ties with the Hebrew

THE CURTAIN FALLS, BUT THE DRAMA HAS JUST BEGUN

Scriptures, but none more so than the book of Revelation. There are 404 verses in Revelation, and 278 of them make one or more allusions to some Old Testament passage. This gives us a good idea of the importance of the Old Testament to the first Christians; it was their Bible, even while the New Testament was coming into existence via the letters of the various apostles and the writing of the story of our Lord in the Gospels. From the point of view that I'm offering in this book, the prominence of the Hebrew Scriptures in the climaxing book of the New Testament demonstrates the sense of a continuing plot line.

But while Revelation makes so many references to other biblical writings, it is very much in a class by itself, because of its dramatic and constant use of symbols. We find this kind of writing occasionally in the Old Testament prophets, especially Daniel and Zechariah, but nothing to be compared with its prevalence in Revelation. Scholars suggest that John used this symbolism so that the enemies of the church wouldn't understand what was being said. No doubt this was a factor in the use of this kind of writing. I think it is also true, however, that a message as powerful as the book of Revelation defies transmittal through ordinary language. Novelists and poets often remind us that some truths are simply beyond customary, factual language; only symbols are powerful enough to carry them. Where in the realm of factual language can you do justice to the ultimate struggle between good and evil, the monstrous quality of evil unleashed, or the grandeur of God's purposes and the final fulfillment of God's plan? When data-words cannot suffice, we turn to symbol-words.

I am always fascinated that the four Gospels never give us any physical description of Jesus—not as an infant, as a twelve-year-old, or as a teacher in his thirties. We don't know whether he was tall or short, the color of his hair or eyes, the features of his face. No wonder, then, that artists—whether Flemish or Italian, English, American, or African—have been inclined to give Jesus the features and often the coloring of their kind of people. It is only in Revelation that he is described, and see how he appears: eyes like a flame of fire, feet like burnished bronze, hair as white as snow, with a voice like the sound of many waters (Revelation 1:14-15).

True to the body of Scripture, we have no picture of God except that the one seated on the throne "looks like jasper and carnelian, and around the throne is a rainbow that looks like an emerald" (4:3). The representative of evil first appears as "a great red dragon, with seven heads and ten horns, and seven diadems on his heads" (12:3). A special agent of evil is "a beast rising out of the sea, having ten horns and seven heads," while still another beast comes out of the earth: "it had two horns like a lamb and it spoke like a dragon" (13:1, 11).

Numbers, too, are used symbolically. Twenty-four elders appear before the throne of God (4:4) and four living creatures (4:6), and later one hundred forty-four thousand "out of every tribe of the people of Israel" (7:4). The number seven appears often, beginning with the seven churches of Asia to whom the "letters" are addressed (1:4; chapters 2 and 3), and later seven golden lampstands and seven stars (1:20), seven seals (5:1), and seven angels with seven trumpets (8:1-2). And of course, twelve—twelve gates in the holy city (21:12) and twelve foundations (21:14), and twelve kinds of fruit on the tree of life (22:2).

Most of these numbers are easy to interpret. In some instances twelve represents the twelve tribes of Israel and in others the twelve apostles, and of course the twenty-four elders represent the combined group. These numbers underline our story's continuing plot: at the plot's consummation in Revelation, the people of Israel and the people of the church are combined in forming the Holy City and the leaders of worship (the twenty-four elders) who attend to God constantly. And of course the 144,000 represent a totality, a completeness—twelve times 12,000. Seven is the biblical number for completeness or perfection (as in seven days, and so forth), and four the number for the whole world, as in the four cardinal directions.

Since the language of Revelation is so dominantly symbolical, I urge you not to look for too many specific applications. If you try to attach particular names and times to these symbols, you invite disappointment. We're inclined to do so because we like to think that all of history finds its meaning in our generation, but this is an ego position that is un-Christian in its spirit and that leads to misinterpretation and misapplication of scripture. God has been at work through all of history and is at work in our time, but whether our time is the point of consummation is really none of our business. What is our business is to minister in the spirit of Christ to the needs of our time.

I suggest that we read the book of Revelation in the way we listen to a piece of classical music, enjoying the total effect without getting lost in the particulars. When we listen to such music, we know that the composer is trying to convey a certain experience or perception for the listener's benefit and that each element of the music leads to that end. But we should, therefore, not give all our attention to the occasional crash of the cymbals, however dramatic that sound may be. We do better to listen for the recurring motifs to see how significantly they are conveyed by the strings, the woodwinds, and the brass in their turns. Because if we become too absorbed in the particulars, regardless of their importance, we will lose both the content and the wonder of the total symphony.

Let's make a quick survey of the book, noting that from the beginning it has to do with the return of Christ and with the establishing of his kingdom (1:5-7). Our Lord was introduced by John the Baptist with the message, "Repent, for the kingdom of heaven has come near" (Matthew 3:2), and Jesus picked up the same theme as he went "throughout Galilee, teaching in their synagogues and proclaiming the good news of the kingdom" (Matthew 4:23). The Bible pictures God's kingdom as the end toward which history is aimed. It's clear both by biblical teaching and human experience that there is opposition to God's kingdom, but that this kingdom will eventually come to pass. Revelation says this in another way when Jesus refers to himself in the first chapter as "the Alpha and the Omega" (Revelation 1:8) and again in the closing chapter: "I am the Alpha and the Omega, the first and the last, the beginning and the end" (22:13). Our story begins with him and it ends with him, and the end is a grand, eternal beginning.

The message of Revelation is addressed to the seven churches of Asia. Students have sometimes interpreted these seven churches as representative of the continuing epochs of church history, concluding of course in their own century. The number seven is significant not for epochs of history, but to indicate that the churches represent the total church, since seven is the biblical number for completeness. From a devotional point of view all of us as individuals and as congregations would do well to read these chapters repeatedly, to see what they can teach us about our shortcomings and our strengths, and to remind us that the church—no matter its failings—is God's institution, constantly redeemed by God's reproof and care.

Chapter 4 introduces us to the body of the book, and it does so in the setting of worship. Worship is the dominant mood of this book. We humans are at our best when we worship well, because in worship we are caught up in the spirit of gratitude and love and we are delivered from self-absorption. Worship that fails to capture such a mood falls short of being true worship. It is significant that the song of chapter 4 celebrates the holiness of God ("Holy, holy, holy, / the Lord God the Almighty, / who was and is and is to come" [4:8]) and God's action as Creator ("You are worthy, our Lord and God, / to receive glory and honor and power, / for you created all things, / and by your will they existed and were created" [4:11]).

At this point, however, Revelation takes a turn that doesn't please our tastes. The consummation of all things begins with judgment. To put it simply, we can't have a right universe without setting matters straight, so we have to clear out history's accumulated debris. Judgment! This act of judgment—actually, a series of judgments—is so important that John "began to weep bitterly because no one was found worthy to open the scroll or to look into it" (5:4). The "worthy" one is then introduced, "the Lion of the tribe of Judah, the Root of David," the one who "has conquered" (5:5). This description takes us all the way back to the book of Genesis, where the tribe of Judah is first given the lion image. As we prepare for the regal figure of the lion to enter, we meet instead "a Lamb standing as if it had been slaughtered" (5:6). The four creatures and the twenty-four elders then "sing a new song" praising the Lamb:

> For you were slaughtered and by your blood you ransomed for God
>   saints from every tribe and language and people and nation;
> you have made them to be a kingdom and priests serving our God.
> (5:9-10)

Revelation is giving us a striking picture. God's Lion is a slain Lamb; God demonstrates power, not by fiat and munitions but by sacrificial love. And yet it is that very bleeding love that brings our universe to judgment.

We will understand the chapters that follow only if we grasp the horror of evil and its particular expression in human sin. Eugene H. Peterson has said it well: "Biblical Christians do not sentimentalize Christ. There is fierceness and militancy here. The world is in conflict; our Christ is the first on the field of battle."[3] We noted long ago in our study that since Eden, our planet has been engaged in a conflict between good and evil. That conflict reaches its fullness in Revelation.

It is marked by horrendous violence. An angel blows his trumpet and "there came hail and fire, mixed with blood, and they were hurled to the earth: and a third of the earth was burned up, and a third of the trees were burned up, and all the green grass was burned up" (8:7). At another point, a third of the sun, moon, and stars were struck, "so that a third of their light was darkened" (8:12). Locusts with "the authority of scorpions" torture the human race for five months (9:3-5); a third of humankind is killed in battle (9:15); and so it goes from one ghastly report to another. I'm quite sure these events and the statistics of destruction and death are meant to be taken symbolically, and that they are intended to convince John and his readers that evil is worse than any ordinary description can convey, and that therefore it must be dealt with in just such a horrendous measure. Do these passages shock and offend? They should. That is their intention. It is as if all the pain and sin and ugliness that our universe has ever known are now being brought to judgment.

This reminds us again that the Bible is not a feel-good book, it is an honest book. It doesn't simply assure us that everything is going to be all right; rather, it tells us how bad the situation is. How bad, specifically? Well, so bad that the only remedy was the death of God's Son; thus, the One who opens the initial scroll of judgment is the Lamb who has been slain.

And what of the beast and his mark? The beast symbolizes the antichrist—that is, the spirit that denies and opposes Christ. We know what that term meant in the first century, at the time Revelation was written. The First Letter of John puts it very simply: "This is the antichrist, the one who denies the Father and the Son" (1 John 2:22). In a sense, therefore, what John said in his day— "many antichrists have come" (1 John 2:18)—is true in every generation. The spirit that denies the Father and the Son is always at work in the world. But Revelation describes a time when that spirit will be uniquely strong and present. Is it possible that Revelation is describing any time when the power of government is committed to the destruction of believers? Perhaps. I suspect that you and I might think so if we lived in one of those periods when such governments were at work, or, if we lived in one of those places where, today, to be a believer is to have one's life in danger.

But the book of Revelation comes at last to the place where the personification of evil, Satan, is forever doomed (20:10), the dead are brought to judgment (20:11-15), and the new heaven and new earth are established:

> See, the home of God is among mortals.
> He will dwell with them as their God,
> they will be his peoples,
> and God himself will be with them;
> he will wipe every tear from their eyes.
> Death will be no more;
> mourning and crying and pain will be no more,
> for the first things have passed away. (21:3-4)

Let me make several connections for us. Our story began in a Garden, where we humans and God were in perfect accord (Genesis 2). It ends in a city, where we humans and God are in perfect accord. An adversary appeared at the very beginning of our story (see Genesis 3), and the adversary is brought to judgment at the end of the story (Revelation 20). There was in the Garden "every tree that is pleasant to the sight and good for food, the tree of life also in the midst of the garden, and the tree of the knowledge of good and evil" (Genesis 2:9). At the end of our story, we immortals have a city where "on either side of the river is the tree of life with its twelve kinds of fruit, producing its fruit each month; and the leaves of the tree are for the healing of the nations" (Revelation 22:2). Early in our story, when the people of Israel were about to flee the slavery of Egypt, they protected their homes from the death angel by sprinkling on each doorpost the blood of a lamb (see Exodus 12:1-28). Now, as the story comes to its climax in Revelation, the finest thing we know about the Holy City is that "the throne of God and of the Lamb will be in it, and his servants will worship him" (Revelation 22:3). So it is that our story comes around to where it began.

One more word. As Revelation ends, the focus is on two subjects. On the one hand, the universe—a new heaven and a new earth. And on the other hand, the individual, by way of a grand invitation: "The Spirit and the bride say, 'Come.' / And let everyone who hears say, 'Come.' / And let everyone who is thirsty come. / Let anyone who wishes take the water of life as a gift" (Revelation 22:17).

You and I should have the same remarkable focus. We should realize that we contribute—want to or not, by action or by inaction—to the great conflict, but at the same time, we have eternal importance for just our own, individual significance.

It's quite a story, this Bible, with quite a plot. It's all about God and our human race. So it's all about God and you.

And this is only the beginning.

---

[1] Henry Sloane Coffin, *Joy in Believing* (New York: Charles Scribner's Sons, 1956), page 68.

[2] Bruce M. Metzger, *Breaking the Code* (Nashville: Abingdon Press, 1993), pages 14–15.

[3] Eugene H. Peterson, *Reversed Thunder*, quoted in *God's Message for Each Day* (Nashville: J. Countryman, 2004), page 226.

127

Study Guide
A Hop, Skip, and a Jump Through the Bible

John D. Schroeder

Chapter 1
In the Beginning, God
Genesis

Snapshot Summary

This chapter provides insights into the creation of the universe and introduces the Grand Eternal Plot, the story of God and of God's relationship with humankind.

Reflection / Discussion Questions

1. Why is the biblical story referred to as "God's story"?
2. What do we learn from the book of Genesis about God and the nature of God?
3. What sorts of questions does the book of Genesis raise for you?
4. What does it mean when we say that God is a communicator?
5. Reflect on / discuss the story of Adam and Eve in the garden, including the serpent's visit. What are your thoughts on this story?
6. In what ways does the story of Adam and Eve show the relationship between temptation and choice?
7. Reflect on / discuss the author's statement that as humans, "we want to believe in something."
8. Reflect on / discuss the author's statement that "God has no perfect persons with whom to work, so it's necessary to use the

best available." Do you feel comfortable comparing yourself with the characters of the Bible in this regard? Why or why not?

9. Name a character from Genesis whose story you particularly enjoy, and share why you chose this person.

10. What new insights about Genesis did you receive from reading this chapter? What additional points or ideas would you like to explore?

Prayer: *Dear God, thank you for creating and caring for this world. Thank you for being a communicator, and for allowing us to be in relationship with you. Open our eyes and our hearts to the story of the Bible, that we may learn more about you, humankind, and ourselves. Amen.*

Chapter 2
The Eternal Plot

Snapshot Summary
This chapter provides an overview of the Bible and the human story.

Reflection / Discussion Questions
1. Is it surprising to you that the Bible has a plot? Why or why not?
2. What are some of the different types of literature found in the Bible? Why are there so many different types?
3. How are the stories in the Bible connected? What do they have in common?
4. How is the Bible a love story?
5. What is meant by the statement, "Those who read the Book in faith become part of the plot"?
6. In what ways were the biblical authors different from one another? What did they have in common?
7. What is known about how the books of the Bible came into their present form?
8. Reflect on / discuss the idea that the humanness of the biblical authors does not diminish "the divine source."
9. What are your thoughts on the "miracles" of the Bible's inspiration and preservation?

10. How was your appreciation of the Bible increased by reading
    this chapter? What points would you like to explore further?

Prayer: *Dear God, thank you for the Bible and for all of the spiritual nour-
ishment it contains. Grant that we may grow in knowledge and faith from
reading your Word. Amen.*

Chapter 3
From Exit to Entrance
Exodus Through Deuteronomy

Snapshot Summary
This chapter focuses on the books Exodus through Deuteronomy,
beginning with the exodus of the Israelites from Egypt and concluding with the death of their leader, Moses, as God's people are about
to enter the promised land.

Reflection / Discussion Questions
1. Describe the situation of the Israelites as this chapter begins.
2. What is meant by the statement, "God uses the playbook of the
   enemy as the instrument of grace"?
3. Reflect on / discuss some of the ups and downs, the twists and
   turns in the life of Moses.
4. What are your overall observations or thoughts about the book
   of Exodus? What questions, if any, does it leave you with?
5. How does the book of Leviticus contribute to the grand plot of
   the Bible?
6. What do we learn from this chapter about the tribe of Levi?
7. Is the sacred etiquette of Leviticus important to us today? Explain.
8. Where does the book of Numbers get its name? What are some
   of the noteworthy stories or people we encounter in the book of
   Numbers?
9. Where does the book of Deuteronomy get its name? In this
   book, what challenges are facing Moses?
10. What can be learned about God's relationship to the human
    race by reading the biblical books discussed in this chapter?

Prayer: *Dear God, thank you for reminding us of your faithfulness, and thank you for the leaders you provide to guide us on our journey. May we always remember and be grateful for the faith of the early believers. Amen.*

Chapter 4
A Flag Is Born
From Joshua to David

Snapshot Summary
This chapter covers the transitions, leaders, and events in the Israelite community following the death of Moses.

Reflection / Discussion Questions
1. What is happening as the book of Joshua begins?
2. Why is it important that the Bible is an honest book, rather than a feel-good book?
3. Who are some of the leaders who stand out in the book of Judges? Give a brief summary of why each was important.
4. What impresses you most about Ruth or about the book of Ruth?
5. Why was Saul a person of great promise? What went wrong?
6. What makes Samuel one of Israel's "towering figures," as the author puts it?
7. Reflect on / discuss the good qualities and the bad qualities of David. What do you admire about David?
8. Why does the author say that with David, Israel's flag was born?
9. If you were to select a favorite book of the Bible from this chapter, which would it be, and why?
10. From the period of Joshua to David, give some examples of how God cared for God's people.

Prayer: *Dear God, thank you giving us these God-seekers who provide the foundation of our faith. Help us to learn from their actions and examples. Amen.*

Chapter 5
The People of the Book
Solomon Through Nehemiah/Esther

Snapshot Summary

This chapter begins with the death of King David, includes the ministry of Elijah and Jeremiah, and ends with the book of Esther and the prophet Nehemiah. The twelve tribes of Israel become divided into two nations, Israel and Judah.

Reflection / Discussion Questions

1. What kind of a ruler was Solomon? In what way was he both wise and unwise?
2. How did Solomon's son, Rehoboam, fare as a leader?
3. If you could meet one biblical character from this chapter, who would you choose, and why?
4. How did the biblical writers judge whether a ruler was "good"? What mattered and what did not matter when it came to making that determination?
5. Reflect on / discuss what is noteworthy about Elijah.
6. Reflect on / discuss the troubles that the northern tribes of Israel faced.
7. What were some of the ups and downs that the southern nation of Judah experienced?
8. How did God demonstrate faithfulness during this time period?
9. Why did the two southern tribes of Judah survive as a nation whereas the ten northern tribes did not?
10. What lessons that apply to us today can we learn from this period of history?

Prayer: *Dear God, thank you for showing us the challenges faced by the early believers, and how they made both good and bad decisions. Help us to remember that you always watch over those who believe in you. Amen.*

Chapter 6
Poets and Philosophers
Job Through Song of Solomon

Snapshot Summary
This chapter looks at the Wisdom literature of the Bible and how faith was shared through philosophy and poetry.

Reflection / Discussion Questions
1. How do poetry and philosophy enhance the unfolding of the biblical plot?
2. What did you learn about biblical poetry from this chapter?
3. What does the book of Job offer to us today?
4. Share a favorite psalm from the book of Psalms.
5. What makes the Psalms such a remarkable book?
6. Give your own overview of the book of Proverbs. What do you like about it?
7. Give a brief description of the book of Ecclesiastes. What are we told about its conclusions?
8. How does the Song of Solomon fit into the Wisdom literature? Why might it seem out of place?
9. How are the Psalms and Proverbs similar to each other? How are the two different?
10. Of all the Wisdom books, which one do you appreciate most, and why?

Prayer: *Dear God, thank you for the poets and philosophers who put their faith into words for the Bible. May we be inspired and our faith strengthened as we read their words. Amen.*

Chapter 7
Truth and Consequences
Isaiah Through Malachi

Snapshot Summary
This chapter looks at the faith and actions of the major and minor prophets.

Reflection / Discussion Questions
1. What are your general thoughts or impressions about the prophetic books of the Old Testament?
2. What important roles did the prophets play in society?
3. How are Isaiah's writings connected to the New Testament? What passage, quoted in the Gospel of Matthew, is Isaiah perhaps best known for?
4. Why is Jeremiah called "the weeping prophet"?
5. What declarations did Jeremiah make that caused him to be unpopular?
6. What roles did Ezekiel serve as a spiritual leader? According to the author, what was Ezekiel's key vision?
7. What inspirational stories are found in the book of Daniel?
8. What made Amos an unusual prophet?
9. What lessons can we learn from Jonah?
10. What additional observations or questions from the books of Isaiah through Malachi would you like to discuss or explore?

Prayer: *Dear God, thank you for those who had the courage and faith to preach about the present and the future. Help us to have courage to correct the injustices and wrongs we see today. Amen.*

Chapter 8
The Plot Takes on New Dimensions
Introduction to the New Testament

Snapshot Summary
This chapter provides an introduction to the New Testament, how it came into being, the books it contains, and how it tells the story of Jesus and his teachings.

Reflection / Discussion Questions
1. According to the author, what circumstances were the Jewish people dealing with during the time period between the Old and New testaments?
2. Why is it remarkable that the writings of the Old Testament survived this period of time?

3. According to the author, who were the three major groups of people that existed at the time Jesus began his ministry?
4. How long did it take to write the Old Testament? the New Testament? How do you think these two very different time spans influenced the character and content of each testament's writings?
5. What issues and events were the writers of the New Testament dealing with and writing about?
6. What were the epistles, and what purpose did they serve?
7. Reread Luke 1:1-3. According to the author, what two things impress us about Luke's words in this passage?
8. According to the author, what were John Phillips's observations regarding, and contributions to, the New Testament?
9. How does the Old Testament differ from the New Testament in story and focus?
10. What does the author say about the authority of the Bible and its role?

Prayer: *Dear God, thank you for the good news of the New Testament. In learning more about it and how it came to be, help us to treasure it even more and to put its teachings to use in our lives. Amen.*

Chapter 9
Good News from Prejudiced Reporters
The Four Gospels

Snapshot Summary
This chapter provides insights into the Gospels of Matthew, Mark, Luke, and John.

Reflection / Discussion Questions
1. How are the four Gospels similar to one another? How are they different?
2. How are the four Gospels similar to biographies?
3. Explain the title of this chapter: "Good News from Prejudiced Reporters."

4. Who was Matthew's intended audience, and how did he tailor his message for this group?
5. What elements of Mark's Gospel seemed to be aimed at his audience of first-century Romans?
6. Explain what is meant by the statement, "The author of this Gospel [Mark] is in a hurry."
7. What is known about Luke? What does Luke do to persuade his Greek audience?
8. What evidence is there that John is writing to a Christian audience?
9. Why might John's Gospel be described as "not for the faint of heart"?
10. Which among the four Gospels is your favorite, or which would you like to learn more about? Give reasons for your answer.

Prayer: *Dear God, thank you for the passionate witness of the Gospels, Matthew, Mark, Luke, and John. May we likewise be passionate witnesses as we share the good news of the gospel with others. Amen.*

Chapter 10
The Church Is Born
The Acts of the Apostles

Snapshot Summary
This chapter covers the arrival of the Holy Spirit, and the successes and failures of the people forming the early church.

Reflection / Discussion Questions
1. Why, according to the author, is it important for Christians to spend time reading the book of Acts?
2. What does the book of Acts tell us about the early Christian church? What role do you think fellowship and the "breaking of bread" played in the early church?
3. What does Acts say about the arrival of the Holy Spirit; what extraordinary things occurred?
4. Reflect on / discuss the good that resulted from the trouble and dissension within the Christian church early in the book of Acts.

5. What does the book of Acts show us about the element of risk as it relates to being a follower of Christ?
6. What similarities and/or differences do you see between the early church and today's church?
7. Reflect on /discuss the idea that "no task in the church is minor." In your opinion, what are the keys to effective church leadership?
8. What sorts of struggles did the early church have regarding church membership?
9. Reflect on / discuss the role the apostle Paul plays in the book of Acts.
10. What does it mean that "Paul came into his faith in Christ by the back door"? What does it mean that we, like Paul, know Jesus Christ by faith rather than by sight?

Prayer: *Dear God, thank you for the gifts of the Holy Spirit and for your church. Help us to appreciate all the centuries of effort and work that have brought us the church as we know it today.*

Chapter 11
Letters to New Believers
Romans Through Thessalonians

Snapshot Summary
This chapter is about some of the letters of the early church, which were written by veteran believers to new believers and which later became part of the New Testament.

Reflection / Discussion Questions
1. Share a time when you received a treasured letter.
2. What was the purpose of the letters written to new believers?
3. What do the letters tell us about the problems within the early church?
4. If not primarily by letter writing, in what ways do we pass along Christian knowledge and teachings today?
5. Share what you know about Paul's letter to the Romans.

6. According to the author, what makes First and Second Corinthians such interesting reading?
7. How is the letter to the Galatians different from the other letters Paul wrote?
8. How does Paul's letter to the Ephesians speak to today's Christians?
9. Why is the letter to the Philippians referred to as "Paul's letter of joy"?
10. What do we learn about the second coming of Christ from First and Second Thessalonians?

Prayer: *Dear God, thank you for all of the believers who shaped the early church. Help us to shape the church today through our words, prayers, and actions. Amen.*

Chapter 12
Letters for the Next Generation
First Timothy Through Jude

Snapshot Summary
This chapter provides more insight into the early church through letters from believers who were determined to share the message of Jesus and expand the church.

Reflection / Discussion Questions
1. What does the author tell us about the tradition and legends that serve as the framework for this portion of the New Testament?
2. How did God's message begin to spread throughout the early church? What sorts of perils were involved?
3. What were the apostle Paul's views regarding the role of women in the church, as expressed in his writing and in his own practices?
4. Why does the author refer to Philemon as "an extraordinary little book"?
5. What topics and issues are covered in Hebrews?

6. What does the letter of James tell us about the relationship between faith and works?
7. Give your own overview of First Peter and Second Peter.
8. What issue does John tackle in his first letter, and why?
9. At the conclusion of the chapter, the author touches on reasons why Christianity has survived throughout the centuries. What are your thoughts on this subject?
10. What additional points or ideas from this chapter would you like to explore?

Prayer: *Dear God, thank you for the care and the love that have been invested in sharing your Word through the ages. Help us to grow stronger in faith because of what we have read and what we have heard. Amen.*

Chapter 13
The Curtain Falls, but the Drama Has Just Begun
The Book of Revelation

Snapshot Summary
This chapter provides some insight into how the end of the Grand Plot is really just the beginning.

Reflection / Discussion Questions
1. What is the status of the Grand Plot as this chapter begins?
2. In his opening remarks, what does the author say about endings?
3. What do we know about the author of the book of Revelation, and the circumstances under which the book was written?
4. Reflect on / discuss the use of symbols and symbol-words in Revelation.
5. How is Jesus described in Revelation 1:14-15? Using your own words or images, how would you describe Jesus?
6. What makes Revelation difficult to understand?
7. What advice does the author offer about how to read and study the book of Revelation?
8. Reflect on / discuss what Revelation says about the battle between good and evil and the final days.

9. What information about the events in the book of Revelation did you find most interesting when reading this chapter? What points or questions from the book of Revelation would you like to explore further?
10. How have your reading, reflection, and discussion of this book personally enriched you?

Prayer: *Dear God, thank you for the opportunity learn more about your Word through the written word of the Bible. Thank you for showing us that the Bible isn't just stories of long ago—it's the continuing, living story of you and of your relationship with us, the human race. Guide us as we seek to know you better and as we go forth to spread the message of your love to others. Amen.*